THE
PATH
OF
PEACE

THE
PATH
OF
PEACE

Dennis C. Bliss

Xulon Press

Xulon Press
2301 Lucien Way #415
Maitland, FL 32751
407.339.4217
www.xulonpress.com

Paperback ISBN-13: 978-1-66285-824-6
Ebook ISBN-13: 978-1-66285-825-3

CONTENTS

INTRODUCTION

We are currently living in a world that King Solomon in his great wisdom described as "...vanity and grasping for the wind. What is crooked cannot be made straight, and what is lacking cannot be numbered" (Ecclesiastes 1:14-15). With this accurate depiction of life today, is it any wonder peace is a commodity in very short supply?

Listen as his father, King David, describes the basic plight of man.

My heart is severely pained within me, and the terrors of death have fallen upon me.

Fearfulness and trembling have come upon me, and horror has overwhelmed me. (Psalm 55:4-5)

After this description David responded with a very human response as he searched for peace - let me run away. It seems he was trying to run from what was robbing him of peace, rather than truly searching for peace.

So I said, "Oh, that I had wings like a dove! I would fly away and be at rest." (Psalm 55:6)

But can we find peace and rest by running away, or do we simply take ourselves with us and continue looking for peace in all the wrong places?

One only needs to glance at the newspaper headlines, watch the evening news on television, or scroll Facebook on your cell phone to see the misery and despair sin has brought to our world, and we, in turn, bring upon ourselves. However, there is good news. Peace is available and ours for the taking, but only as we come to know the Lord Jesus Christ as our personal Savior and then are obedient to His Word. David came to this same conclusion and gave us many clues to *The Path of Peace* when he decided not to "run away" but to seek God.

As for me, I will call upon God, And the LORD shall save me. Evening and morning and at noon I will pray, and cry aloud, And He shall hear my voice.

He has redeemed my soul in peace...(Psalm 55:16-18a)

It is my sincere desire the words that follow will truly lead you on *The Path of Peace.*

CHAPTER 1

THE DEFINITION OF PEACE

I f we are to journey on *The Path of Peace*, then we need to know our final destination and describe the route to take in order to successfully assure a safe arrival. Our final destination, of course, is "peace", and the route will be described in chapter six. Thus, our starting point must be a definition of peace that will give us both the destination goal and an understanding of our journey as well.

You may not think this is necessary, but listen to this quote from one of my counseling clients. "I am afraid of peace." As I recovered from the shock of that statement, I asked why he would ever be afraid of peace. His reply: "because after peace comes the storm." You see, his problem was with his definition of peace. For him, the word only meant "absence of trial, trouble, turmoil, or tribulation". In other words when nothing upsetting was going on. So, lest others have similar or other definitions, we need to define exactly what is meant in this book by the word "peace".

Webster's New World Dictionary offers their first definition for the word peace as "freedom from war". However, this is not the sense in which we are considering peace. This definition would only apply as we possibly think about freedom from war within our own soul and spirit, or freedom from war with Almighty God (James 4:4), or with Satan.

To turn to some more spiritual definitions and better ideas of what peace really is, we find the following:

1

Vine's Expository Dictionary sees peace as "the inner sense of rest and contentment resulting from the reconciliation of one's spirit to God."

Wilson's Old Testament Word Studies presents peace as being "secure, tranquil, at rest".

Unger's Bible Dictionary defines it as "...outward conditions of tranquility ...spiritual peace through restored relations of harmony with God."

Or, as I once heard an old preacher describe it: "peace is the total realization of and reliance upon God's intention for your life."

Generally when you read the word "peace" in this book, we will be talking about a deep inner bosom peace. A sense of knowing and feeling, deep within our heart, soul, and mind, that is undisturbed by circumstance. Undisturbed because of the faith awareness that God is in control, and that any circumstance is always for His glory and for the good of those who love Him (Isaiah 43:7/Romans 8:28). Please read on and find "wisdom" for "her ways are ways of pleasantness, and all her paths are peace" (Proverbs 3:17). The God-directed path leads to a peace "which surpasses all understanding" (Philippians 4:7). Read in peace and find peace.

CHAPTER 2

THE KINDS OF PEACE

The word "peace" means many different things to many different people; and even in Scripture the word takes on varied meanings. As we consider the kinds of peace, the largest single distinction would primarily have to do with the origin of that peace. The two main kinds of peace available to us are that which the world gives (worldly), and that which comes from God (godly).

People constantly search every day for peace to calm the fears and frustrations of their daily lives, and as we shall see, they need to look in the right place (i.e. the right Person, chapter three) to find full and final satisfaction for their troubled souls. Since most of us are more earthly than heavenly-minded, we tend to search the world first for our lasting peace. However, we all find the same result as did Solomon when he discovered that "all is vanity and grasping for the wind" (Ecclesiastes 1:14).

The world basically pursues activity or busyness as the means to ease a troubled mind. Athletic endeavors, study courses on relaxation, books, television, radio, Facebook, etc., are all used to get our minds off of our problems through distraction or entertainment. Some men and women work hard at their jobs and hobbies, hoping against hope that mere busyness will calm their troubled souls. Others turn to chemical substances such as drugs and alcohol to escape from the horrible reality that appears to be theirs. Some look for solace in love and raw sex, but, alas, these too fall short in their ability to bring peace.

In fact, look with me at the Scriptural descriptions of what we really can expect to find as results from a pursuit of peace in the common so-called worldly "peacemakers."

PLEASURE

> He who loves pleasure will be a poor man ...
> (Proverbs 21:17a)

It takes a great deal of expense to maintain the lusts of sensuality because they are truly insatiable. They do not bring peace, but poverty and the emotional strain of financial ruin and unsatisfied desires. So, I must spend more money looking for a different avenue, hoping this one will bring peace. Forgive the worldly expression but looking for peace in pleasure reduces one to "champagne tastes on a beer budget."

Even King Solomon in all of his wisdom and finances found that pleasure was not able to bring satisfaction or peace.

> I said in my heart, "Come now, I will test you with mirth;
> therefore enjoy pleasure"; but surely, this also was vanity.
> I said of laughter–"Madness!" and of mirth, "What does it
> accomplish?" (Ecclesiastes 2:1-2)

ALCOHOL (and drugs)

What about booze/drugs? Can't they bring me peace, or at least relief from reality? Maybe if I get drunk/high enough I can be at peace. Maybe just a couple drinks/pills to take the edge off. Maybe, just maybe!

> Who has woe? Who has sorrow? Who has contentions?
> Who has complaints? Who has wounds without cause? Who
> has redness of eyes?
> Those who linger long at the wine, those who go in search
> of mixed wine.

Do not look on the wine when it is red, when it sparkles in
the cup, when it swirls around smoothly;
At the last it bites like a serpent, And stings like a viper.
Your eyes will see strange things, And your heart will utter
perverse things.
Yes, you will be like one who lies down in the midst of the
sea, or like one who lies at the top of the mast, saying:
"They have struck me, but I was not hurt; they have beaten
me, but I did not feel it. When shall I awake, that I may seek
another drink?" (Proverbs 23:29-35)

Sounds like despite the drinking, woe, sorrow, contention, complaints, wounds all are still present. So as the passage ends, I need another drink. Does this sound like the description of a person who has found peace?

Yet another unmerciful consideration, alcohol/drugs only contribute to spending more and more money in the search for peace with the end result of "he who loves wine and oil will not be rich" (Proverbs 21:17b).

WORK

Hard work is one of the things that is admired as a good trait in our society. In fact, if you are considered to be well-steeped in the "Puritan work ethic", you would be considered a good person, a valuable employee, a good friend. And yet, many work for two reasons which have nothing to do with "ethic", but are really means to find peace. Some (so-called workaholics) work to get away from the realities of life and attempt to find peace in the hours and effort they put into their labors. Others work for the financial gain (riches) and the "peace money can buy".

But can hours and hours of work bring peace? Can concentrating on work really drown out one's troubles and trials? Can I work hard enough to be so tired my mind will not be able to think of those things which rob me of my peace? Solomon found all of this to be lacking and ineffective as "peace-makers". He readily recognized the law of diminishing returns when it comes to worldly attempts to find peace.

All the labor of man is for his mouth, and yet the soul is
not satisfied. (Ecclesiastes 6:7)

Even in hard work and long hours there is nothing for the heart and soul. Natural desires return every day, day-after-day, never to be satisfied. The true desires of the soul find nothing in this world to give them satisfaction; thus, no peace can be found here.

Then I looked on all the works that my hands had done and
on the labor in which I had toiled; and indeed all was vanity
and grasping for the wind. There was no profit under the sun.
(Ecclesiastes 2:11)

Solomon realized that to search for peace in labor was an unending and unfulfilling process, for man is never satisfied. "There is no end to all his labors, nor is his eye satisfied with riches" (Ecclesiastes 4:8). And thus, the lack of peace from hard work brings us to our next worldly "peacemaker".

RICHES

Will you set your eyes on that which is not? For riches
certainly make themselves wings; they fly away like
an eagle toward heaven. (Proverbs 23:5)

He who loves silver will not be satisfied with silver;
nor he who loves abundance, with increase. This also is
vanity. (Ecclesiastes 5:10)

Talk about the "eagle flying". There is nothing more transitory and unfulfilling than financial gain. There is never enough; there must always be more. In fact, when a well-known billionaire was asked how much money would be enough, his response was "one more dollar". Never satisfied, never fulfilled, peace, not here "for one's life does not consist in the abundance of the things he possesses" (Luke 12:15).

In fact, we find not only will riches fail to bring peace, they cannot even insure one of a good night's rest for "the abundance of the rich will not permit him to sleep" (Ecclesiastes 5:13). Tossing and turning, turning and tossing. Thoughts of how to keep what he has; thoughts of how to gain more; thoughts of how to spend it to gain the peace he cannot find.

God's Word goes even further to show that not only can riches not bring the desired peace, but they may in fact add to the miseries of this worldly life.

> There is a severe evil which I have seen under the sun:
> riches kept for their owner to his hurt. (Ecclesiastes 5:13)

> He who trusts in his riches will fall, but the righteous will
> flourish like foliage. (Proverbs 11:28)

> A man with an evil eye hastens after riches, and does not
> consider that poverty will come upon him. (Proverbs 28:22)

FRIENDS

> Confidence in an unfaithful man in time of trouble is like a
> bad tooth and a foot out of joint. (Proverbs 25:19)

A toothache and a foot out of joint sounds more painful than peaceful. Friends are imperfect and will fail us. That brings not peace, but pain and even reluctance to lean on them in time of trouble. This is not like the peace of assurance God gives which is unquestionable confidence in the knowledge God is in control.

Okay, so maybe friends can fail, but what about people in general? Surely, we could find someone to assist in our quest for peace. If you think this is true, listen to King David as he concludes that "the help of man is useless" (Psalm 108:12).

> Look on my right hand and see, for there is no one who acknowledges me; refuge has failed me; no one cares for my soul. (Psalm 142:4)

In fact, David begins to see the real source of permanent peace when he states:
It is better to trust in the LORD than to put confidence in man. (Psalm 118:8)

MUSIC

Many look for peace in music. Some use the volume and beat in an attempt to drown out that which is interrupting their peace. Others find a bit of solace in the soothing strains of good, wholesome music. In fact, there is a biblical precedent that indicates there can be some measure of peace to be found in music.

> Let our master now command your servants, who are before you, to seek out a man who is a skillful player on the harp. And it shall be that he will play it with his hand when the distressing spirit from God is upon you, and you shall be well. (I Samuel 16:16)

The text goes on to indicate in verse 23 that there was refreshment and a return to good mental health; but in I Samuel 18:10-11 we see the results were temporary and really depended on the attitude of the listener. So, music can help, but it is not a long- term open door to peace.

KNOWLEDGE

Still others attempt to quiet the uneasy voices within them by study - the pursuit of knowledge. Hours of reading and maybe even memorization, intense thought, and in-depth analysis - all trying to bring some measure of peace to a troubled soul. We will again, as always, look to Scripture, but even Shakespeare realized that "much learning doth make thee mad", not bring you peace.

> For in much wisdom is much grief, and he who increases knowledge increases sorrow. (Ecclesiastes 1:18)

> And further, my son, be admonished by these. Of making many books there is no end, and much study is wearisome to the flesh. (Ecclesiastes 12:12)

Truly, one can become tired from study, but only physically. No amount of study, no matter how long, no matter how hard, can be enough to bring peace to the heart and soul.

SEX

> Harlotry, wine, and new wine enslave the heart. (Hosea 4:11)

Sexual encounters, even accompanied by alcohol, cannot bring peace. Why? Because the sexual experience was designed by God as part of the "one flesh" experience (Genesis 2:24). It was reserved exclusively for a man and his wife. Anything outside of those God-given boundaries brings problems (not peace) to a life. Those who commit illicit sexual intercourse come away with confusion as they seem to have brought that sexual partner somehow into the very core of their lives. The result is much like going outside on a morning when the temperature is twenty below zero, wetting your tongue and sticking it to a metal flagpole. You are right; it will freeze fast, and nothing you can do will remove your tongue from that cold, cold metal without painfully leaving a little bit of it stuck there torn from your tongue. So it is with sex; each encounter leaves a little of you with your partner and vice versa.

Thus, it should be easy to see sexual uncleanness infatuates and weakens people. It takes away sensitivity, robs them of understanding, brings confusion (not the peace they were seeking), and takes the heart away from any consideration of God. The inherent consequence: without God there is absolutely no possibility for real peace (Isaiah 57:21).

With all of these attempts trying to find peace in this world, it soon becomes evident that peace cannot be found here outside of God's provision for peace. In fact, Dr. David Jeremiah puts it this way in his book *The Book of Signs*. "We are living in a world where anything goes, but nothing satisfies."

To summarize the search for peace in all of these worldly fashions, the Old Testament prophet Jeremiah speaks twice of the fleeting and transitory nature of the world's peace in chapter six and verse fourteen and again in chapter eight and verse eleven.

> They have also healed the hurt of My people slightly, Saying,
> "Peace, peace!" When there is no peace.

Thus, the peace of the world gives temporary relief at best, continual return to frustration and misery at worst. It gives a promise of peace, but no substance or lasting effects or respite from the mental anguish and emotional chaos.

Worldly peace simply attempts to soothe people in their sin, giving them drugs or activity to make things somehow easier. Yet with all of this, Jeremiah's people recognized and admitted the fallacy of looking for peace in all the wrong places.

> We looked for peace, but no good came; and for a time of
> health, and there was trouble! (Jeremiah 8:15)

Some time later, the people add to this admission the reason they cannot find peace in worldly things.

We acknowledge, O LORD, our wickedness and the iniquity
of our fathers, for we have sinned against You. (Jeremiah 14:20)

I believe the problems with searching for peace in a worldly fashion can be summed up in two very simple statements.

1. Man is a sinful creature, incapable of finding or experiencing peacebon his own. He is insatiable.

    …the eyes of man are never satisfied. (Proverbs 27:20b)

2. Anything or anyone other than God which pretends to offer peace becomes a "god" to the seeker, and only brings temporary relief, not real peace.

Their sorrows shall be multiplied who hasten after another god.
(Psalms 16:4a)

Having seen the fallacy and shortcomings of worldly peace, we turn our attention to real peace - Godly peace. In God's Word, the word "peace" is found over four hundred times. Here again there are many different kinds of peace that are mentioned and following is a sampling of some of those various kinds of peace.

National/societal peace - the absence of war
Peace with each other - the absence of personal conflict
Hold thy peace - an admonition for silence
Peace be unto you - a personal salutation
Go in peace - a personal farewell
Going to the grave in peace - a final farewell
World peace - the millennium

However, these are not the kinds of Godly peace we are considering. The types of peace in which we are most interested are the prerequisite peace - peace WITH God (Chapter Four) and, the resulting bosom "peace that passes understanding" - the peace OF God (Chapter Five).

CHAPTER 3

THE PERSON OF PEACE

Before considering the peace **with/of** God, we must first meet the person and source of all peace - the Lord Jesus Christ, the beloved Son of God. The prophet Isaiah gives us an introduction to the person of peace that seems to turn the Old Testament focus toward the personal inner peace we are considering.

> For unto us a Child is born, unto us a Son is given;
> and the government will be upon His shoulder. And His
> name will be called Wonderful, Counselor, Mighty God,
> Everlasting Father, **Prince of Peace**.
> Of the increase of His government and peace there
> will be no end...(Isaiah 9:6, 7, emphasis mine)

Along with this prophecy of His coming and who He is, Isaiah also prophesied how Jesus would establish our peace **with** God and pave the way for the peace **of** God.

> But He was wounded for our transgressions, He was
> bruised for our iniquities; the chastisement for our peace
> was upon Him, and by His stripes we are healed. (Isaiah 53:5)

> All of this was necessary because:
> All we like sheep have gone astray; we have turned,
> every one, to his own way; and the LORD has laid on

Him the iniquity of us all. (Isaiah 53:6)

According to the Apostle Paul, Christ has reconciled us to God and brought us peace with Him through His suffering on the cross, which took away the binding power of the law and removed the enmity between us and God.

> For He Himself is our peace, who has made both one,
> and has broken down the middle wall of separation,
> having abolished in His flesh the enmity, that is, the
> law of commandments contained in ordinances, so as to
> create in Himself one new man from the two, thus making
> peace,
> and that He might reconcile them both to God in one
> body through the cross, thereby putting to death the enmity.
> And He came and preached peace to you who were afar
> off and to those who were near. (Ephesians 2:14-17)

Paul goes on to tell us the specific agent of peace that God chose to use, was the precious blood His son shed on the cross of Calvary.

> And by Him to reconcile all things to Himself, by Him,
> whether things on earth or things in heaven, **having made
> peace through the blood of His cross.** (Colossians 1:20,
> emphasis mine)

Since we have already discussed the fallacies of worldly peace, you will notice in the preceding verse that Christ has it within His power to bring peace with/of God here on earth as well as in heaven. In fact, He goes on to promise an eternal personal peace to those of us who choose to accept His offer.

> Peace I leave with you, My peace I give to you; not as
> the world gives do I give to you. Let not your heart be troubled,
> neither let it be afraid. (John 14:27)

14

Further, He goes so far as to offer us words of cheer in spite of the warning there would be much tribulation in the world as we walk through our lives.

> These things I have spoken to you, that in Me you may
> have peace. In the world you will have tribulation; but be
> of good cheer, I have overcome the world. (John 16:33)

Thus, through Christ we have peace **with** God, and so in Him we have peace in our hearts and minds (the peace **of** God). What an occasion to have good cheer. This word (cheer) means to be of good comfort: to take heart in the fact all will be well. In spite of the tribulations of this world, we are to be of good cheer, to keep our hope and delight in God regardless of the circumstances and situations around us. Because of this, Paul could say *we glory in tribulations* (Romans 5:3); and James could echo that we can *count it all joy when we fall into various trials* (James 1:2), and *blessed is the man that endures temptation* (James 1:12).

Christ says the foundation of this peace is the fact *I have overcome the world* (John 16:33). This is a fact and promise that extends to those of us who know Him as our personal Savior.

> For whatever is born of God overcomes the world.
> And this is the victory that has overcome the world–
> even our faith. (I John 5:4)

Is it any wonder Christ can make this great personal invitation to us for "peace with God" and "the peace of God"?

> Come to Me, all you who labor and are heavy laden,
> and I will give you rest.
> Take My yoke upon you and learn from Me, for I am
> gentle and lowly in heart, and you will find rest for your
> souls.

For My yoke is easy and My burden is light. (Matthew 11:28-30)

Even if we go back in history, back to the Old Testament, long before he realized Christ was the true source of peace, David knew at least that its true source was God.

> Then they cried out to the LORD in their trouble, and
> He delivered them out of their distresses. ...
> For He satisfies the longing soul, and fills the hungry
> soul with goodness. (Psalm 107:6, 9)

In addition to this, listen to the benediction which the Apostle Paul leaves us. Now may the God of hope fill you with all joy and peace in believing, that you may abound in hope by the power of the Holy Spirit. (Romans 15:13)

And lastly, listen as David expounds on the blessed results in one's own life that comes with the realization 'the person of peace" is the ONLY one who can bring true peace into our lives. His peace is the sort of peace which allows for a good night's rest even in times of trouble.

I will both lie down in peace, and sleep; for You alone,

O LORD, make me dwell in safety. (Psalm 4:8)

I had felt the above verse was indeed the conclusion of this chapter, until my wife and I recently visited a small Mennonite country store. What caught my eye and heart was a sign in the window which pointedly and succinctly provides a very effective summary of the relationship between peace and "The Person of Peace."

NO JESUS,
NO PEACE!
KNOW JESUS,
KNOW PEACE!

CHAPTER 4

THE PEACE WITH GOD

In our search for inner peace you might be wondering, "Why do we need peace with God?" Isn't He a God of love who will let us all fellowship with Him for eternity? What does peace "with" God have to do with our personal inner peace anyhow? The answer is SIN; we are sinners and therefore separated from God, His love, and the peace that He alone can give.

For all have sinned and fall short of the glory of God, (Romans 3:23)

But your iniquities have separated you from your God; And your sins
have hidden His face from you, So that He will not hear. ...
(Isaiah 59:2)

Isaiah goes on to describe how this separated condition affects our ability to have peace of any kind when he says:

The **way of peace they have not known**, And there is no justice in
their ways; They have made themselves crooked paths; Whoever
takes that way **shall not know peace**. (Isaiah 59:8, emphasis mine)

In very plain words, because of sin we are a wicked people, which
precludes us from being a people of peace or at peace.
But the wicked are like the troubled sea, When it cannot rest,

Whose waters cast up mire and dirt. "**There is no peace**,"
Says my God, "for the wicked." (Isaiah 57:20-21, emphasis mine)

As already stated, our sin and wickedness have separated us from
God and have left us in a state that the Bible describes as being at
ENMITY with God. The word "enmity" is an old English word that
according to Mr. Webster means: "the bitter attitude or feelings of
an enemy or of mutual enemies; hostility, antagonism. It denotes a
strong, settled feeling of hatred, whether concealed, displayed, or latent."
Scripture completely agrees with this definition as Paul states in his
Epistle to the Romans.

Because the carnal (sinful, wicked) mind is enmity against God;
for it is not subject to the law of God, nor indeed can be.
(Romans 8:7, insertion mine)

The writer James echoes this truth, and very strongly adds to it the
idea that even our search for peace in the world rather than at the feet
of the "Person of Peace" puts us at enmity with almighty God.

Adulterers and adulteresses! Do you not know friendship with
the world is enmity with God? Whoever therefore wants to be a
friend of the world makes himself an enemy of God. (James 4:4)

Thus, even people searching for peace can be at odds with God,
and a great gulf exists between God's love and sinful people. That gulf
could only be bridged by the precious Son of God and His shed blood,
for "without shedding of blood there is no remission of sins (Hebrews
9:22). And yet, it was this "Prince of Peace",

Whom God set forth as a propitiation by His blood, through faith,
to demonstrate His righteousness, because in His forbearance God
had passed over the sins that were previously committed.
(Romans 3:25)

Going back to the very beginning of creation, man was created to have perfect fellowship and communion (and, thus peace) with God his Creator. Man's sin changed all of that and brought about a separation, a tearing apart of the relationship. To put things back the way they were intended necessitated a reconciliation, a binding together of that which was broken. The Greek word "eirene" means "bound together", it re-establishes peace with God and opens the door for "the peace of God". Therefore, it should come as no surprise that "eirene' is the word translated as "peace" many times in the New Testament. In fact Christ uses this word when He says to us:

Peace (eirene) I leave with you, My peace (eirene) I give to you; not as the world gives do I give to you. Let not your heart be troubled, neither let it be afraid. (John 14:27, insertion mine)

So, we can see peace is always born out of reconciliation, always comes to us from God, and is always through the "Prince of Peace", the Lord Jesus Christ. Paul bears this thought out in his letter to the Corinthians.

Now all things are of God, who has reconciled us to Himself through Jesus Christ...(II Corinthians 5:18)

God, and God alone, could make this reconciliation possible, because we as "enemies" have no interest in reconciling with God because "there is none that seeks after God" (Romans 3:11). "And the way of peace have they not known" (Romans 3:17). Therefore, before the foundation of the world, God instituted a plan to restore the relationship between Himself and man and establish *The Path Of Peace*. This path led His precious Son to the cross at Calvary where He would shed His life's blood as the binding agent of reconciliation.

For if when we were enemies we were reconciled to God through the death of His Son, much more, having been reconciled, we

shall be saved by His life.
And not only that, but we also rejoice (at peace) in God through
our Lord Jesus Christ, through whom we have now received the
reconciliation. (Romans 5:10-11, insertion mine)

And by Him to reconcile all things to Himself, by Him, whether
things on earth or things in heaven, having made peace through
the blood of His cross.
And you, who once were alienated and enemies in your mind by
wicked works, yet now He has reconciled. (Colossians 1:20-21)

That was God's part, to provide the path for mankind to walk toward,
and find, *The Path of Peace* and reconciliation. But what about our part
you may ask? Is there something we must do? Our responsibility and
part in this divine plan is truthfully summed up in a verse of Scripture
written by the prophet Isaiah hundreds of years ago.

Let the wicked **forsake** his way,
And the unrighteous man his thoughts;
Let him **return** to the LORD,
And He will have mercy on him; And to
our God, For He will abundantly pardon.
(Isaiah 55:7, emphasis mine)

So, as you can see, our "peace with God" is somewhat of a joint
effort - God's part was to prepare the way and pave it with the blood
of Christ, mankind must take the step to walk the path, and that is a
step of "faith".

Therefore, having been justified by faith, we have **peace with God**
through our Lord Jesus Christ. (Romans 5:1, emphasis mine)

CHAPTER 5

THE PEACE OF GOD

Once we have established "peace with God", we may begin to appropriate the "peace of God" in our daily lives as we face temptations, struggles, and tribulations that would undermine the inner peace we so much crave. To truly remain calm in the midst of the storm; to not be depressed, distressed, anxious, or fearful; to not be controlled by our circumstances; all these desires tug at the very fabric of our deepest emotional being. We are desperately looking for inner peace; that deep, safe, secure feeling that is undisturbed by circumstance or personal situation.

Maybe you wonder if you already posses this "peace of God" or question whether you even need it. Are there ways to indicate if I am at peace or not? How will I know? Following are a few things to consider, which are fairly good indications you do not have "the peace of God".

- Certain situations or people make you feel anxious.
- You are prone to worry and fretting.
- You get discouraged and give up easily.
- People often tend to disappoint you.
- have a very critical and/or cynical spirit.
- The things you have do not satisfy, and you want more.
- You are prone to losing your temper.
- You can be happy one moment, then "down' the next.
- You have bad feelings or hold grudges against other people.
- Life's small annoyances trouble you more deeply than they should.
- You are not even thankful for what God has done for you, and are not thankful for what you have.

If any, especially many, of these statements are true in your life, you do not have "the peace of God".

Even the God-fearing King, King Hezekiah, had many of these same questions perplexing him after a time of great sickness. He felt as if he were going to die and going to hell, felt as if his bones were all breaking, was filled with mourning, felt oppressed, and was resigned to "walk carefully all my years in the bitterness of my soul" (Isaiah 38:9-15). All of these feelings were coming to him at a time when he realized he should have been at peace. Listen as he comes to his great personal discovery about the "peace of God".

Indeed it was for my own peace that I had great bitterness;
But You have lovingly delivered my soul from the pit of corruption,
For You have cast all my sins behind Your back. (Isaiah 38:17)

Shouts of joy! He has found the key and unlocked the door to the "peace of God". He has discovered the primary truth that the "peace **of** God" begins with "peace **with** God". Which is the joy of "sins forgiven", the happy state of eternal reconciliation to God. Praise God!!! I can be at peace; you can be at peace because our eternal destiny has been forever settled by almighty God Himself. Bask with me as our souls experience peace in the knowledge of what God has done with, and how He feels about, our sin, once we have accepted the Lord Jesus Christ as our personal Savior.

- Our sins are cast behind his back (Isaiah 38:17).

-He has chosen not to remember our sins (Jeremiah 31:34, Isaiah 43:25, Hebrews 8:12 and 10:17).

- He has blotted out our sins in a thick cloud (Isaiah 44:22).

- He has removed our sins as far as the east is from the west (Psalm 103:12).

- He has cast our sins into the depths of the sea (Micah 7:19).

Thus, the first aspect of the "peace **of** God" is possessing "peace **with** God". Inner peace begins with and is the effect of the forgiveness of our sins resulting in full reconciliation to God.

But you ask how does my salvation guarantee me peace? I have "peace with God", but what about my circumstances? Can God supply peace in any and every situation? To answer those questions, one needs only to listen to King David in Psalm 55 where David's enemies and false friends were causing him much grief. Observe the setting:

My heart is severely pained within me, And the terrors of death
have fallen upon me.
Fearfulness and trembling have come upon me, And horror has
overwhelmed me. (Psalm 55:4-5)

That does not sound very peaceful. Sounds more like some terrible circumstances. But listen as David shares the stunning results.

He has redeemed my soul **in peace** from the battle (circumstances)
that was against me, For there were many against me. (Psalm 55:18,
emphasis and insertion mine)

David's circumstances were weighing him down with emotional pain, worry, anxiety, fear, even trembling. He prayed and the answer from God was PEACE. Peace in the midst of the storm. David felt a calmness of spirit from God, almost as if nothing was wrong. That peace, the "peace of God", is yours too, if you have "peace with God". Listen to this promise from God delivered by the apostle Paul to young Timothy:
For God has not given us a spirit of fear, but of power and
of love and of a sound mind. (II Timothy 1:7)

How much more peace could we have than to possess a "sound mind" Sound (at peace) because it is stayed upon the Rock Jehovah and His Son.

> You will keep him in perfect peace, whose mind is stayed on You, Because he trusts in You. (Isaiah 26:3)

We can look around at our circumstances; looking back at the past with anger, guilt, regret, or we can look to the future with worry and anxiety, or we can look up to the One who is in control and works "all things for our good" and find peace. I call this type of thinking the "one way arrow" - an arrow pointed straight at the throne of grace where peace is found.

In fact, thinking about this principle and the "good" of Romans 8:28, I am reminded of a story I heard which bears directly on this issue. We do not necessarily get what we "want", but we will always get that which brings us closer to God and His peace.

> One Sunday morning at a small southern church, the new pastor called on one of his older deacons to lead in the opening prayer. The deacon stood up, bowed his head and said, "Lord, I hate buttermilk". The pastor opened one eye and wondered where this was going. The deacon continued, "Lord, I hate lard". Now the pastor was totally perplexed. The deacon continued, "Lord, I ain't too crazy about plain flour, but after you mix 'em all together and bake 'em in a hot oven, I just love biscuits".
> "Lord help us to realize that when life gets hard, when things come up that we don't like, whenever we don't understand what You are doing, that we need to wait and see what you are making. After you get through mixing and baking, it'll probably be something even better than biscuits. Amen!

Sounds like that old deacon has found the essence of peace - simply trusting his life and all its circumstances to his Lord and Savior. How about you???

We may also have "the peace of God", not only because we have "peace with God", but also because God through His Son, the Lord Jesus Christ, has bequeathed us peace. In John 14 we are told twice "let not your heart be troubled" (verses 1, 27), because God has given us His own personal peace. In fact, the whole chapter contains many things which bring peace to our troubled hearts as we reflect on what God is telling us.

- Verses 1-3 Peace comes from the knowledge that God is preparing a place of peace as our eternal home.

- Verse 6 Peace comes from the knowledge that God prepared a way of reconciliation through His Son.

- Verses 7-12 Peace comes from the knowledge that Christ is God, thus everything He has promised is true and available to us.

- Verses 13-14 Peace comes from the knowledge that our prayers will be answered according to His will.

- Verses 15- 26 Peace comes from the promise and presence of the indwelling Holy Spirit of God.

- Verse 27 Peace comes as a direct result of a personal bequest from Christ - it is a GIFT!

In verse 27 when Christ says "peace I leave with you", He goes on to say "My peace I give to you". Herein are established two very precious and important doctrinal truths.

1. MY PEACE - it is the very peace of God, Himself, that is being imparted to us. Think of it, the peace of God within us for

our use; to meet all of our needs and available for all of our circumstances.

2. I GIVE UNTO YOU - like salvation, it is a free gift, and the "gifts and calling of God are irrevocable" (Romans 11:29).

Then placed between these two truths is a third truth that is very important to our concept of the peace God gives. Christ explains that His peace is "not as the world gives". His peace is not the transitory, fleeting peace of the world, but is permanent and able to meet every need. It is, in fact, a "peace that passes understanding" which "will guard your hearts and minds" (Philippians 4:7). Is it any wonder Christ ends John 14:27 with these words of peace and comfort? "Let not your heart be troubled, neither let it be afraid."

Bask in the words of one (King David) who has found "peace with God" and is now resting in the "peace of God". Let his thoughts bring you peace as you not only read, but understand that if you know Christ as your personal Savior, these words are true for you as well.

The LORD is my shepherd; I shall not want.
He makes me to lie down in green pastures;
He leads me beside the still waters.
He restores my soul; He leads me in the paths of
righteousness For His name's sake.
Yea, though I walk through the valley of the shadow
of death, I will fear no evil; For You are with me; Your
rod and Your staff, they comfort me.
You prepare a table before me in the presence of my
enemies; You anoint my head with oil; My cup runs over.
Surely goodness and mercy shall follow me All the days
of my life; And I will dwell in the house of the LORD Forever.
(Psalm 23)

What a peaceful picture. Is that where you are? If not, seek God's peace.

CHAPTER 6

THE PATH OF PEACE

As we have seen, the "path of peace" has as its first step the establishment of "peace with God". Many have said this is as simple as "A,B,C". I would agree it is simple, but I believe the Biblical formula for salvation and peace with God is A+B+C+R.

A - ADMIT
One must admit he/she is a sinner, and as such is powerless to save himself/herself.

For all have sinned and fall short of the glory of God. (Romans 3:23)

B - BELIEVE
This next step toward peace is really a step of faith in Jesus and His atoning work.

That if you ...believe in your heart that God has raised Him from the dead, you will be saved. (Romans 10:9)

C - CONFESS
Confession means to agree with God about our sin and to then acknowledge it verbally to God.

That if you confess with your mouth the Lord Jesus and believe in your heart that God has raised Him from the dead, you will be saved. For with the heart one believes unto righteousness, and with the mouth confession is made unto salvation. (Romans 10:9-10)

R- REPENT

Repentance is "a change of mind, with sorrow for something done, and a wish that it was undone". (Smith's)

I tell you, no; but unless you repent you will all likewise perish.
(Luke 13:3)

Have you made "peace with God"? If not, why not do it right now? You will find it is impossible to find peace in this world without being reconciled to the God of peace. It is really as easy as A+B+C+R. All you need to do is to bow your head and ask the Lord Jesus to be your Savior and give you "peace with God" so you can also have the "peace of God".

Believing and praying something like the following will bring both peace **with** God and the peace **of** God.

Dear God,
I admit I am a sinner without hope of saving myself.
I repent of my sins and do hereby confess them. I believe that Jesus Christ is your Son who came to die, who was buried and resurrected to pay the penalty for my sins. By faith I now ask Him to be my personal Savior and bring me peace with you and to give me your peace in my life. Amen!

Once this step of faith that begins "the path of peace" is taken care of, we are ready to journey according to God's leading. As you view the road map to peace, you will begin to understand that even though peace is a gift from God, its maintenance or daily provision is more dependent upon our attitude and conduct than our circumstances. This is so vital that I want to repeat it with emphasis so you do not miss the point. **OUR PEACE IS MORE DEPENDENT UPON OUR ATTITUDE AND CONDUCT THAN OUR CIRCUMSTANCES.**

We will be seeing in order for us to have peace, there is much action needed upon our part. There is much for us to do as we "follow after" or "pursue" peace in our daily lives, in all our circumstances, and in all situations of life.

For instance, in II Corinthians 11:24-28 we see the apostle Paul was beaten, stoned, shipwrecked, snake bit, in many perils, weary, full of pain, hungry, thirsty, cold, naked, and had the burden of the oversight of all the churches. Does that sound very peaceful to you? And yet, with all of this, Paul discovered peace, or rather LEARNED how to have peace.

Not that I speak in regard to need, for **I have learned** in whatever state I am, to be content (at peace).
(Philippians 4:11, emphasis and insertion mine)

What peace! Content in any circumstance, any situation. If you think this came easily to Paul, or simply as a free gift, think again. Paul had to learn how to be content (be at peace). Unlike us, Paul did not have the completed Bible to glean from and thus had to stumble and feel his way along "the path of peace" under the guidance of the Holy Spirit. For us the path can be so much simpler and easier as we have the complete road map at our disposal.

We have previously mentioned that the first step toward the "peace of God" is to have "peace with God" because as the old song goes, "you can't have one without the other". This is born out in the book of Proverbs where we find:

Happy is the man who finds wisdom, And the man who gains understanding. (Proverbs 3:13)

because,

Her ways(wisdom) are ways of pleasantness, And all her paths are peace. (Proverbs 3:17, insertion mine) and,

> The fear of the LORD leads to life, And he who has it
> will abide in satisfaction (peace)…
> (Proverbs 19:23, insertion mine)

According to Psalm 111:10 wisdom is the "fear of the Lord", or in plain English, it is salvation. Once again we find the first step on the path of peace is a step of faith, for "we are saved by grace through faith" (Ephesians 2:8), or as simply put by Christ: "...your faith has saved you, go in peace" (Luke 7:50).

As you have read these Scriptures, I trust you have noted the various words which God has chosen to use: "way, path, and go" - all denoting a definite direction laid out for us and definite action (go) to be taken on our part. At this point I believe it would be prudent to be reminded that **OUR PEACE IS MORE DEPENDENT UPON OUR ATTITUDE AND CONDUCT THAN OUR CIRCUMSTANCE.** So come with me as we look for the signposts which direct us on our journey to and along the "path of peace".

In the world of psychology, a cognitive psychologist is one who basically believes that what goes on in the mind controls the feelings and actions of the individual, and would therefore, postulate that the first signpost on the path of peace would be in the mind. It appears God would agree with this premise for He states:

> For as he thinks in his heart, so is he…(Proverbs 23:7a)

Thus, the first item of conduct toward peace is to make sure we conduct our minds in a peaceful manner. Isaiah gives us a clear direction as he points the direction arrow toward God Himself.

> You will keep him in perfect peace, Whose mind is
> stayed on You, Because he trusts in You. (Isaiah 26:3)

This peace, this perfect peace, is both safe and easy. It is a holy security and serenity of mind coming from the assurance of God's favor for the one who trusts God at all times, in all situations, in every set of circumstances. It is peace because "to be spiritually minded is life and peace"(Romans 8:6b). This is the blessing which comes to the righteous man whose trust is in the Lord.

> He will not be afraid of evil tidings; His heart is steadfast,
> trusting in the LORD. (Psalm 112:7)

> Not only will fear be gone, but there is also the promise
> that we will be "happy".
> Happy are the people who are in such a state; Happy are
> the people whose God is the LORD! (Psalm 144:15)

> Happy is he who has the God of Jacob for his help,
> Whose hope is in the LORD his God. (Psalm 146:5)

I believe it was these types of comfort and security in the peace that God can give which prompted Frances Ridley Havergal to pen one of the great old hymns of the faith, "Like a River Glorious". Let the words of the chorus get down into the very depths of your soul to reveal the peace that comes from staying our hearts and minds upon Almighty God.

> "Stayed upon Jehovah, Hearts are fully blest -
> Finding as He promised, Perfect peace and rest".

However, since our critical and cynical minds will wonder if and how long this peace can last, Isaiah goes on to inform us we can trust in God **forever** - right through this life on into eternal life.

> Trust in the LORD forever, For in the LORD,
> is everlasting strength (and peace). (Isaiah 26:4, insertion mine)

But, how does one know God or even begin to trust Him, to "stay his mind "on Him in the pursuit of peace? God has chosen one way and one way alone to reveal Himself to us, and that is through His Word. Therefore in order to have peace, we have to spend time in His Word as an integral part of the conduct of our mind. Check it out in God's Word!

> **Great peace** have those who love Your law, And **nothing** causes them to stumble. (Psalm 119:165, emphasis mine)

Since God cannot be separated from His Word, it is not hard to understand that one must search for peace in God and find it in the pages of His Word. Peace becomes the blessing for those who not only love the Word of God, but for those whose lives are also ruled by that Word of God. Abundant satisfaction, and therefore peace, comes from reflecting on and obeying this Word, which was given "for our learning, that we through the patience and comfort of the Scriptures might have hope" (Romans 15:4). In stark contrast, a love of the world, attempting to find peace in the world only brings "vanity and grasping for the wind" (Ecclesiastes 1:14).

Beware, however, a cursory reading of God's Word will not suffice in the quest for peace. In fact, we are commanded over and over again in Psalm 119 to "meditate and delight" in the Word of God. The word 'meditate' could be interpreted "ruminate", like a cow chewing her cud. Taking it in, chewing it, swallowing it, gaining nourishment from it, and bringing it back up again when more nourishment is needed. We must not only "read" what God is saying, we must "listen".

> I will hear what God the LORD will speak, For He will speak peace To His people and to His saints…(Psalm 85:8)

But doesn't listening come easily? Since God speaks in a "still, small voice" (I Kings 19:12), we need to stand still, stop what we are doing, and pay attention to what God's Word has for us. What He is offering us in Himself and in His Word, is PEACE. Contained in this verse is a reminder that "the peace of God" is only available after "peace with God" (i.e. only to His people, His saints). For "to be spiritually minded is life and peace"(Romans 8:6b), and a mind can only be spiritual if it is "stayed upon" God and His Word. King David found this true in his own life.

> This is my comfort in my affliction, For Your word
> has given me life. (Psalm 119:50)

We must "stay" our minds on God's Word; we must "listen" to its words; and, we must "walk" in the Word as well. In fact, the word "walk" has to do with the conduct of our daily lives, speaking of our obedience, which we will discuss in greater detail later in this chapter. Suffice it here to note, if our conduct is according to the Word of God, the result is peace as promised.

> And as many as walk according to this rule, peace
> and mercy be upon them...(Galatians 6:16)

Along with salvation, peace also comes as a gift - one of the fruits of the Spirit. In fact, as you review each of the spiritual gifts recorded in Galatians, you will notice each one contributes to our overall ability to have peace.

> But the fruit of the Spirit is love, joy, peace, longsuffering,
> kindness, goodness, faithfulness,
> gentleness, self-control. Against such there is no law.
> (Galatians 5:22-23)

LOVE - a sacrificial "agape" love as seen in I Corinthians 13:4-8

JOY - cheerfulness in life, a constant delight in God

PEACE - with God and in conscience, a peaceful temper and behavior towards others, undisturbed by circumstances

LONGSUFFERING - patience to defer anger and to endure trials

KINDNESS - sweetness of temper, courteous with others

GOODNESS - readiness to do good to all

FAITHFULNESS - with what we have, profess, promise and do

GENTLENESS - not easily provoked

SELF-CONTROL - moderation in the exercise of our appetites

So, you can readily see not only are we given "peace", but each of the other fruits greatly contribute to , increase the magnitude of, and enhance our ability to have peace.

The last point I would like to make about "staying our minds", is that we are allowed to think about other things but must be careful we do not think about things which will rob us of our peace. We are so prone to think about the cares of this everyday world, and because of sin we are pretty well negatively charged. (Check out the "black dot" in chapter 8.) Therefore, Paul gives us another signpost for our minds and the direction our thoughts should take if we wish peace.

> Finally, brethren, whatever things are true, whatever things are noble, whatever things are just, whatever things are pure, whatever things are lovely, whatever things are of good report, if there is any virtue and if there is anything praiseworthy–meditate on these things.
> The things which you learned and received and heard and saw in me, these do, and the God of peace will be with you.
> (Philippians 4:8-9)

Do you see any negative possibilities here? Any room for peace-destroying thoughts? This is a New Testament reminder that "we are what we think" (Proverbs 23:7). So if we think right, that is, think peacefully, we will have peace.

Also take note of a very small word in verse 9 - **do**. It is a word of obedience which brings the promise of God's peace. The word is in the military command mode and also carries with it the idea not of a one time action, but an ongoing action which builds in strength, application and results through its repeated efforts. More doing (right-thinking, prayer and supplication) brings more and more peace.

Preceding this admonition to "think right", the apostle Paul furnishes us with another signpost on "the path of peace". This signpost has two directional arrows pointing in the same direction, but with different wording on the signs - one a caution, the other a remedy. The caution - do not worry; the remedy -prayer and thanksgiving.

> Be anxious for nothing (don't worry), but in everything
> by prayer and supplication, with thanksgiving, let your
> requests be made known to God;
> and **the peace of God**, which surpasses all understanding,
> will guard your hearts and minds through Christ Jesus.
> (Philippians 4:6-7, insertion and emphasis mine)

Paul recognized that worry was one of the greatest enemies (Chapter 8) of peace because it clouds the mind and decreases the mind's ability to be "stayed upon" God or His Word. Since the impact of worry on our peace will be dealt with later, we will only mention it here as a caution.

On the positive side of the quest for peace, the most effective way of unloading our minds and getting them back to the anchor of our souls is prayer, or as Paul puts it: prayer, supplication, and thanksgiving. "Prayer is the expression of man's dependence upon God for all things" (Unger). Supplication is "asking for favor in some special necessity" (Unger). Thanksgiving is "gratitude for all the benefits of divine Providence" (Unger). Given these definitions, it should be easy to see how these things in and of themselves lend peace to the heart and mind. An acknowledgement of the "all sufficient grace" of God (II Corinthians 12:9), and faith in His ability to "supply all your needs" (Philippians 4:19) can bring calm to any troubled soul. Simply put, prayer forces the mind to "stay" upon God and thus bring peace; not just peace, but a "peace that passes understanding" (Philippians 4:7).

The result is our hearts and minds are kept through Christ Jesus. This reminds us that our peace comes from the "person of peace". But what are we "kept" from? This peace keeps us from sinning under the weight of our troubles, keeps us from sinking under them, keeps us from worry, and keeps our hearts and minds "stayed" upon God, and God alone. See David's comment on the effectiveness of prayer as a readily available peace-bringer.

> I called on the LORD in distress; The LORD answered
> me and set me in a broad place. (Psalm 118:5)

This "broad place" is a quiet haven of peaceful rest and security.

As briefly mentioned earlier, obedience is also one of the directions that is pointed to by the signposts directing us along "the path of peace". In fact, it can easily be said obedience is the key to all of the blessings of life that God has in store for us (Hebrews 10:36). Again, it is our conduct that is at issue rather than our circumstances. Listen to some of the challenges found in the Word of God regarding obedience and its relationship to peace.

> Thus says the LORD: "**Stand** in the ways and **see**,
> And **ask** for the old paths, where the good way is,
> And **walk** in it; Then you will find rest for your souls.
> (Jeremiah 6:16, emphasis mine)

Stand, look, see, and then walk - all action (conduct). The term "walk" equals obedience which brings complete rest for the weary soul.

The first thing we need to believe, as explained earlier, is that God is the source of peace.

> God is our refuge and strength, A very present
> help in trouble. (Psalm 46:1)

We must believe His Word holds the key and is the only road map to peace.
> For whatever things were written before were written
> for our learning, that we through the patience and
> comfort of the Scriptures might have hope. (Romans 15:4)

So now we turn to some of the other principles found in God's Word that are able to bring peace into our daily lives, **IF** we truly believe them. For example, when it comes to suffering, we need to believe:

> For our light affliction, which is but for a moment,
> is working for us a far more exceeding and eternal
> weight of glory. (II Corinthians 4:17)

> For I consider that the sufferings of this present time
> are not worthy to be compared with the glory which
> shall be revealed in us. (Romans 8:18)

We also must cling to this great promise:

> And we know that ***all things*** work together for good
> to those who love God, to those who are the called
> according to His purpose. (Romans 8:28, emphasis mine)

It needs to be mentioned here that "those who love God" are those who are obedient. This is an idea that is stressed by the Lord Jesus, Himself in such verses as:

> If you love Me, keep My commandments. (John 14:15)

We need to believe that in times of trial, tribulation, and temptation God is there, will not allow the situation to be more than we can bear, and will always give us a "way out".

> No temptation has overtaken you except such as is
> common to man; but God is faithful, who will not
> allow you to be tempted beyond what you are able,
> but with the temptation will also make the way of
> escape, that you may be able to bear it.
> (I Corinthians 10:13)

Come to think of it, most of us in our human frailty want just that - a way out. We want to avoid any pain or any inconvenience that we possibly can. Yet God's way many times is to give us what we need to go through the situation, much as He protected the three Hebrew children in the fiery furnace, or Daniel in the lion's den (Daniel 3 & 6). Listen as Paul discovered this scriptural principle.

> And He said to me, "My grace is sufficient for you,
> for My strength is made perfect in weakness."
> (II Corinthians 12:9a)

With this knowledge, belief, and trust in God's Word, Paul could go on to comment:

> Therefore most gladly I will rather boast in my infirmities,
> that the power of Christ may rest upon me.
> Therefore I take pleasure in infirmities, in reproaches,
> in needs, in persecutions, in distresses, for Christ's sake.
> For when I am weak, then I am strong. (II Corinthians 12:9b-10)

This is what Paul had "learned" (Philippians 4:11) - to take pleasure in, to "be content" with those uncomfortable circumstances and situations in which he found himself. What a place of peace!

We simply need to believe in the power of God, and that He provides the power to us to bring peace into our lives.

> I can do all things through Christ who strengthens me.
> (Philippians 4:13)

> For God has not given us a spirit of fear, but of **power**
> and of love and of a sound mind (complete peace).
> (II Timothy 1:7, emphasis and insertion mine)

Not only do we have to believe in the power of God, but we must also believe in His provision. Either He is able to bring us peace, or He is not. However, it is not His ability that is in question, but our ability to truly believe in and obey His Word. Once again, what we believe influences our ability to find peace. How can we not have peace if we believe the following revelation from God through the apostle Paul.

> And my God shall supply **all your need** according
> to His riches in glory by Christ Jesus.
> (Philippians 4:19, emphasis mine)

Because of the word "riches", a cursory glance at this verse would seem to indicate that God is only interested in meeting our financial or material needs. But what does the word "all" mean? Just that - ALL! If we are to believe God will meet all of our needs and that His grace is truly sufficient, can we help but have peace in our hearts?

I am a fisherman and over the years have cast thousands of live or artificial baits at hopefully hungry fish. There is an axiom involved here that would go something like this - you can't catch a fish if you don't cast bait. This is much like "the path of peace" - you can't have peace if you hold onto those things which destroy your peace (see Chapter 8). Or, put into more positive terms - you get peace by casting your circumstances to the Lord. Christ loved fishermen and taught them lessons about belief and action which is possibly why God put this step on "the path of peace" in fisherman's terms.

> Cast your burden on the LORD, And He shall sustain you; He shall never permit the righteous to be moved.
> (Psalm 55:22)

> Casting all your care upon Him, for He cares for you.
> (I Peter 5:7)

Since you may not be a fisherman, you may not know what casting is. It is throwing out the bait to a spot that you believe will have good results. So, this casting is simply turning over to God those things which are robbing us of our peace. It is giving Him the responsibility for supplying sufficient grace and meeting our needs for those things which upset and worry us - rob us of our peace.

Notice it is **upon Him** that we are to cast our burdens, not ourselves. The word cast indicates that we cast it like fish bait with a rod, not a yo-yo which keeps bringing it back. It is also interesting in the Greek that verses 6 and 7 are actually one sentence, thus tied together. Therefore, there must be some connection worth our consideration. So, verse 6 says

> Therefore humble yourselves under the mighty hand of God, that He may exalt you in due time. (I Peter 5:6)

Why would we need to humble ourselves before casting our burdens and care upon the Lord? Well think about it. Aren't we the ones trying to fix, change, worry about, etc. the situation, and thus are feeling worried, fearful, anxious? Come to think about it, look at the middle letter of the following words:

> guilt
> grief
> worrisome
> anxiety
> anxious
> pride

That's right "**I**" - right smack in the middle. "**I** can't fix, change, control this, so **I** am worried, fearful, anxious, etc." In other words, not so spiritual terms really meaning - "**I** don't trust God." We need to get out of the way and give (cast) the circumstance to Him, **for He cares for you**. Get out of the way and truly "cast" all your care upon Him.

Another step on this road is also another action word. If we want peace we need to follow it, to pursue it, to study and **do** those things which make for peace. In other words, we can't simply wish for it and talk about it. WE MUST SEEK IT! This should be very understandable since we all see peace as a very illusive commodity which we seem to be chasing constantly anyhow.

> Therefore let us **pursue** the things which make for peace
> and the things by which one may edify another.
> (Romans 14:19, emphasis mine)

The writer of Hebrews echoes this idea as well.

> **Pursue** peace with all people, and holiness,
> without which no one will see the Lord:
> (Hebrews 12:14, emphasis mine)

Thus, it would seem that following after peace is not only good for us, but also our duty. Our duty to keep ourselves reconciled, with one another, regardless of our status as wrongdoer or the party having been wronged. Reconciliation once again can be seen as part of the fabric of peace.

If we are to follow this peaceful path, we will find our destination to be a peaceful, restful haven under God's protection and care.

> ...my soul trusts in You; And in the shadow of Your
> wings I will make my refuge, Until these calamities
> have passed by. (Psalm 57:1b)

So, dear friend, casting our burdens and following "the path of peace" puts us directly on the course where God can supply ALL our needs and apply His all-sufficient grace to our situation. Certainly, there we find a refuge, a haven, a place of peace.

Since we must also concern ourselves with the "whole counsel of God", we need to understand that to just simply follow is not enough. There are several other actions necessary to keep us on "the path of peace".

> **Flee** also youthful lusts; but **pursue** righteousness, faith,
> love, peace with those who call on the Lord out of a pure heart.
> (II Timothy 2:22, emphasis mine)

According to I Peter 2:11 those lusts "war against the soul" - hardly a prescription for peace. Therefore, Paul explains to young Timothy that peace also results from how fast and how far we run away from lust towards lives of righteousness.

The apostle Peter also presents much the same picture as far as finding other actions to go along with the pursuit of peace.

> For "He who would love life And see good days,
> Let him refrain his tongue from evil, And his lips from
> speaking deceit.

> Let him **turn away** from evil and **do good**; Let him
> **seek peace and pursue it**. (I Peter 3:10-11, emphasis mine)

It would appear that avoiding evil and doing good are also steps along the way to contentment, happiness, and peace. Our duty appears to be to seek peace rather than division and contention. David realized the same process on "the path of peace" several thousand years ago when he wrote:

> Depart from evil and do good; Seek peace and pursue it.
> (Psalm 34:14)

Thus, it should be easy to see God's path to peace includes departing from evil, guarding our tongues, which will help keep peace with those around us by avoiding strife and contention, doing good, and seeking (following, pursuing) peace. In other words, keep yourself right, have a peaceful disposition, don't break the peace, and study others and situations to determine the things which produce peace. At this point you may be asking yourself about the benefits of all this which sounds much like a lot of hard work. Listen as David extols the virtues of "following" the path God's way.

> I sought the LORD, and He heard me, And delivered
> me from all my fears. (Psalm 34:4)

> … those who seek the LORD shall not lack any good thing.
> (Psalm 34:10b)

You probably have also noticed there has been a great deal of emphasis on "doing good". However, this should not come as a surprise since:

> …we are His workmanship, **created** in Christ Jesus **for good
> works**, which God prepared beforehand that we should walk
> in them. Ephesians 2:10 (emphasis mine)

We only need to go to the Word of God and see the result (peace) that comes, if we but choose to live our lives in the manner God intended. But glory, honor, and peace to everyone who **works what is good** … (Romans 2:10, emphasis mine)

This relationship between "doing good" and the resulting peace can be very well demonstrated by a piece of prose written a few years ago, by a dear retired pastor friend of mine who has since entered into his final, eternal peace. Listen as he displays how our conduct rather than our circumstances deliver peace.

A WONDERFUL EXCHANGE

I trudged down a long, a painful, weary road;
My nerves were taut,
My mind an endless maze of worries,
Each task a burden too great to bear.
T'was then I heard a brother call my name;
With feet of lead and heart of stone
I turned aside in answer to his plea.
How low he lay, How agonizing was his cry,
How pained his head not knowing
what to do or say.
My brother think upon Gethsemane
And Calvary's dark despair.
Now Jesus can give strength and peace
To such as you and me!
And as I prayed for this dear one,
My burden great and dark was lifted.
The sun rose warm and bright upon my road,
For in helping another I was helped;
In giving, I too was given the peace and
joy of the Lord.

by Rev. Charles F. Foster

Hand-in-hand with "doing good" is the concept of righteousness, or what we might simply describe as "right-living". It is living in obedience to and in accordance with the Will and Word of God. David aptly describes this relationship of peace with righteousness in Psalm 85:10b as "righteousness and peace have kissed each other." Isaiah had described this symbiotic relationship approximately two centuries earlier when he said:

> The work of righteousness will be peace, And the
> effect of righteousness, quietness and assurance forever.
> My people will dwell in a peaceful habitation, In secure
> dwellings, and in quiet resting places.
> (Isaiah 32:17-18)

Sounds rather peaceful, doesn't it? In the doing of our duty, as God has revealed it, we will find abundance of true pleasure, quietness and assurance to the end of time. What we are promised here is holy serenity and security of mind, which the world has not the power to give, nor the power to destroy. The outward manifestation of this inward peace is dwelling in quiet, restful (peaceful) places regardless of circumstance.

There is an English word which has changed considerably in its meaning since the King James translation in 1611. The word that has undergone this profound transformation is the word MEEK. Today most of us would resent being referred to as meek, or as the phrase might possibly go - meek and mild. The modern connotation is of a "Casper Milquetoast" character; one who is a "timid, shrinking, apologetic person" (Webster). In fact, to call someone "meek" today could very well disrupt the peace with a fist in the nose. However, when King James authorized his translaton of the Scriptures the word had a much more spiritual meaning to it as "one yielded to God's authority", or "one who would rather suffer wrong than to do wrong, and thereby enjoy God's favor" (Smith). With this definition in mind it is easy to understand how meekness and peace go together!

> But the meek shall inherit the earth, And shall delight
> themselves in the abundance of peace.
> (Psalm 37:11)

This is an easy conclusion to reach since the "meek" are the most contented with what they have, who they are, and are thus not easily disturbed. They are truly those who have:

> Great peace have those who love Your law, And nothing
> causes them to stumble. (Psalm 119:165)

In fact, the whole pursuit of peace could be summed up like this: salvation (peace with God), then spiritual growth, and spiritual growth brings greater peace (the peace of God). The Bible says we are to notice, even copy, the spiritually mature, upright man for "he shall enter into peace" (Isaiah 57:2a), the end result of his ways is literally peace.

> Mark the blameless man, and observe the upright;
> For the future of that man is peace. (Psalm 37:37)

Put another way, God's reward or benefit to the faithful is peace of heart, mind, and soul. But as it is with God's blessings, there are conditions we must fulfill, and/or gifts we must appropriate.

> Commit your works to the LORD, And your thoughts
> will be established.
> ... When a man's ways please the LORD, He makes
> even his enemies to be at peace with him.
> (Psalm 16:3, 7)

In summary, I believe the key to "the path of peace" can be found in one word -

OBEDIENCE - obedience to the will and Word of God. First being obedient to salvation's call, and then to the call for obedience. It is only in obedience to all of the road signs which point the proper way to the peaceful destination where one can reach that final peaceful resting place, both in this life and life hereafter.

> For you have need of endurance, so that **after you have done** the will of God, you may receive the promise.
> (Hebrews 10:36, emphasis mine)

So simply put, there it is - God promises peace (John 14:27), and "the path of peace" is obedience as seen in the above verse. We have seen that it can be fruitlessly searched for in the world or successfully in God's Word, and we will find (Chapter 8) there are many ways in which we can destroy our peace or hinder God's ability to supply it as He has promised. Listen to the blessed condition of one who has searched for peace and has been obedient to God's Word.

> Blessed is the man Who walks not in the counsel of the ungodly, Nor stands in the path of sinners, Nor sits in the seat of the scornful;
> But his delight is in the law of the LORD, And in His law he meditates day and night.
> He shall be like a tree Planted by the rivers of water, That brings forth its fruit in its season, Whose leaf also shall not wither; And whatever he does shall prosper.
> (Psalm 1:1-3)

What a simple and yet profoundly beautiful portrait of "the path of peace", showing the source (God), the map (knowledge of and obedience to His Word), the peaceful picture (planted tree), the provision (rivers of water), the purpose (to bring forth fruit), the permanence (leaf shall not wither), and the resulting peace (he shall prosper). My heart and pen can only echo the words of praise uttered by the psalmist so many, many years ago.

> Oh, that men would give thanks to the LORD for His goodness, And for His wonderful works to the children of men! (Psalm 107:8)

The promise of peace is there; the path has been revealed: "This is the way, walk in it" (Isaiah 30:21).

CHAPTER 7

THE PRODUCTS OF PEACE

Most of "the products of peace" come as a result of walking on "the path of peace" and are therefore by-products of following the path God has laid out as His prescription for peace. These by-products will result in both inner and outer manifestations of peace in the heart.

First of all, we will look better. Peace in the heart brings a smile to the face, a skip to the step, a sparkle in the eye, and a note of music to the voice.
"A merry heart makes a cheerful countenance."
Proverbs 15:13a)

How can we help but look better when we know all is right with the world because it is going according to God's plan, at least within our hearts. We have peace "with" God and peace "from" God which not only sustains us but uplifts us as well. Should we not at least look calm and serene, if not downright happy? The problem is that many of us "sit, soak, sulk and sour, looking like we were baptized in lemon juice". That does not portray the light of the gospel, or our professed belief in God's Word to those around us like "peace in the midst of a storm" does.

Another outward physical manifestation of inner peace is a good night's rest. There is no tossing and turning, no insomnia of the heart, for the heart is at peace. There is just the ability to lay your head on the pillow and a short while later be in deep, deep, peaceful sleep.

"I will both lie down in peace, and sleep; For You alone,
O LORD, make me dwell in safety." (Psalm 4:8)

As you see this person is not alone, for God is with him and protects him. He can enjoy himself because he commits all his affairs to God, leaves all troubling issues aside, and casts them upon the Savior. Is it any wonder he can rest so peacefully at night?

If we move to the inner man, we will see that doing what God requires brings not only peace, but also many side benefits and blessings. Righteousness is not only a prerequisite for peace, but also an end result of peace. If we are at peace, it is easier to live righteously, and if we live right, we get peace.

"Now the fruit of righteousness is sown in peace by those
who make peace." (James 3:18)

We can surmise from this verse how inner qualities emphasize peace in the life in two ways. First, righteousness is sown (has its origins) in the peaceful inner conditions of one's life. Second, righteousness appears as a living quality in those who practice peace. In short, we could say peace depends upon obedient Christian living, and Christian living depends upon peace.

If you remember, the first step on "the path of peace" is a step of faith which brings salvation. The Old Testament (especially in the Proverbs) refers to this as "getting wisdom" and as such brings some very peaceful dividends. One of those is what we might call a "state of happiness", for:

"Happy is the man who finds wisdom, And the man who
gains understanding." (Proverbs 3:13)

and,

"He who heeds the word wisely will find good, And
whoever trusts in the LORD, happy is he."
(Proverbs 16:20)

The word translated here as "happy" could just as easily have been translated as the word "Blessed". Knowing God is in control of our circumstances and knowing He "blesses" us adds to peace, and at the same time is also a product of peace. This comes because we are walking "the path of peace" with its assurance of God's protection, provision, and promise that "all things work together for good" (Romans 8:28). We see the by-products of walking this path, which spring from peace, are abundance of delight and the ability to be satisfied with life as it is because God is in control.

> "Her ways (wisdom's) are ways of pleasantness, And
> all her paths are peace." (Proverbs 3:17, insertion mine)

Since we become God's children through this act of salvation, listen to some of the other products which come along with peace.

> "The LORD will give strength to His people; The
> LORD will bless His people with peace." (Psalm 29:11)

The strength, here mentioned, is for several purposes: strength to enable good works, strength to fortify against evil, strength to resist trials and temptations, and, yes, even the strength to walk "the path of peace." As we utilize this strength to do God's will, God even gives us another unique by-product to add to our inner peace.

> "When a man's ways please the LORD, He makes even
> his enemies to be at peace with him." (Proverbs 16:7)

Think of that; God not only brings us peace but also helps insure peace by bringing our enemies into a state of peace with us. No wonder God wants us to 'love our enemies" (Matthew 5:44). Love and peace - what a "peaceful" picture and prospect for our lives.

There are multitudinous benefits or blessings from being a child of God, but I will mention just one last direct product of being able to be called "my people", because of knowing Christ. This following promise relates specifically to the millennial kingdom, but I do not believe I am using too much license to apply it to the current issue, for certainly inner peace brings a certain blessing upon the state of our family home as well.

> "My people will dwell in a peaceful habitation, In secure dwellings, and in quiet resting places." (Isaiah 32:18)

If one is at peace with God, at peace with himself, and at peace with the family, can there help but be peace, quiet, and rest in the home? Could this be one of the aspects of the old hymn mentioning "blessed quietness"?

On "the path of peace", we also found one of the steps was to know God's Word. This too brings other products which are part of peace, but also contribute to other benefits as well. For instance,

> "Great peace have those who love Your law, And nothing causes them to stumble." (Psalm 119:165)

This indicates a people not bothered by circumstance, because they are not offended (or upset) by people or situations. Why? Because they are God's people, and they are steeped in His Word, they have faith and trust in His Word, and, thus, they have a sense of holy security and understanding that "all things work together for good" (Rom. 8:28).

If you are like most of us, you have first tried to find peace everywhere else except from God and His path. The real pavement of His path is His Word. Thus eventually we must all finally begin to pray and search the Scriptures much like the Psalmist of old.

"I thought about my ways, And turned my feet
to Your testimonies (Word)".
(Psalm 119:59, insertion mine)

Once we finally and futilely exhaust all other possibilities, we return to God's Word and find peace was always there, ready for us. Also along with peace comes the realization that His Word can also bring comfort to our troubled hearts. Again, we see this amazing relationship: peace brings comfort, comfort aids peace. God's Word supports us, lifts us up in our affliction.

"Unless Your law had been my delight, I would then
have perished in my affliction." (Psalm 119:92)

God's Word also teaches us how to comfort ourselves in time of trouble. The idea here being the Word of God can impart to us the ability to be undisturbed by our circumstances.

"This is my comfort in my affliction, For Your word
has given me life. ...
I remembered Your judgments of old, O LORD,
And have comforted myself." (Psalm 119:50, 52)

Some years ago this was made very real and personal to me. I was in the middle of the two largest trials of my life, and though it seemed like all of life would come crashing down upon me, God did send inner peace and grace sufficient to meet my every need. What I learned was God was indeed very real. He was faithful to His Word, and also, if I obediently followed His path as described in His Word, His promises could be applied to my life. Basically, my trials brought me closer to His Word, which brought me closer to Him, which in turn not only brought peace, but a new and different look at His will for my life. It taught me the priceless lesson of God's faithfulness and my love of and obedience to His Word could see me through any and all adversity. It was at this point that I adopted a new verse of Scripture as my life's verse.

"It is good for me that I have been afflicted, That I may learn Your statutes." (Psalm 119:71)

Isn't it amazing how even when we profess to have faith in God and His promises, when there are trials and troubles we cringe. Maybe even get a bit angry when someone quotes Romans 8:28 to remind us "all things work together for good". At that moment we think of this verse as some sort of inane platitude or trite saying which does not bring us peace. I don't know if the following story is true or not, but it greatly emphasizes the truth of God's promise.

A man was involved in a shipwreck and was the sole survivor. He clung to a piece of the ship and drifted to a small deserted island. Upon reaching shore, he gathered items from the wreck and proceeded to build himself a small shelter for protection from the elements. One day while searching for some food he glanced back in the direction of his shelter only to see it burning. He rushed to the scene but all was lost - his food, clothes and other items necessary for his survival. He sunk down in the sand and cried, "Lord why would you let this happen to me? Shipwrecked, and now my only means of survival have perished as well." That night he crawled into the brush and spent the night tossing and turning without much sleep. Shortly before dawn he drifted asleep, but soon was awakened by voices he thought were

coming from the beach. Am I dreaming?
But no, those were real voices. He got
up and ran to the beach, and there found
men and a boat. He asked them what they were
doing there. Their response - "we've come
to rescue you." But how did you know
I was here? "WE SAW THE SMOKE
FROM YOUR SIGNAL FIRE!"

Despite the tragedy, despite the danger, despite the heartache, despite the trial, did things work for good?

So, we have already seen peace allows us to dwell in quiet resting places, but I failed to mention the size of those places. Some would accuse God of doling out tiny bits of His grace and blessings, but my God "is able to do exceedingly abundantly above all that we ask or think "(Ephesians 3:20). Listen as David describes the size of the resting place which God provided for him (and for us as well):

"I called on the LORD in distress; The LORD answered
me and set me in a broad place." (Psalm 118:5)

This verse teaches us three wonderful truths. First, we must call, which is part of finding the path. Second, God is faithful and ever-present to meet our need. And third, He will supply us with even more peace than we can imagine or even deserve in that "broad place."

The last category of "the products of peace" is somewhat different, for the previous things have for the most part related to the benefits gained from our inner peace. These last two products come from our inner peace and result in an outworking of our peace for the benefit of others. At this point you may be wondering how our inner peace can outwardly benefit other people any more than we are simply nicer people to be around. Remember "The Wonderful Exchange" back in chapter Six? Also consider these two peaceful duties of a child of God:

witnessing/soul winning and counseling. Aren't they much easier and more readily attempted when we are at peace?

Look at the Old Testament description of the priest who had walked "the path of peace":

> "The law of truth was in his mouth, And injustice
> was not found on his lips. He walked with Me in
> peace and equity, And **turned many away from
> iniquity**." (Malachi 2:6, emphasis mine)

In the New Testament, even the armor of God brings a preparation, a readiness to adhere to, abide by, and proclaim the gospel, which brings both "peace with God" and the "peace of God". For God has "shod your feet with the preparation of the gospel of peace" (Ephesians 6:15).

So once again we see the gospel brings peace, and peace brings the gospel. How neatly God has planned and fit it all together. So much so, He chose to describe the feet of one who brings peace as "beautiful" (Isaiah 52:7 and Romans 10:15).

This brings us to the last product of peace, my life's vocation of counseling. Certainly as you sit across the desk you would want to know there is inner peace in the life of your counselor. If his/her mind were cluttered by their own trials and temptations, what good could they hope to do for you? What kind of example of applying the truth of God's Word to their lives would they be? But peace goes far beyond a mere platform from which to counsel, it is a solid foundation borne from a God-given responsibility.

> "Blessed be the God and Father of our Lord
> Jesus Christ, the Father of mercies and God
> of all comfort,
> who comforts us in all our tribulation,
> **that** we may be able to comfort those who
> are in any trouble, **with the comfort with
> which we ourselves are comforted by God**."
> (II Corinthians 1:3-4, emphasis mine)

So, this is a process of exercise and growth much like the training methods undergone by weightlifters. They stretch and strain their muscles with more repetitions and greater weight loads in order to prepare for the future. God thus stretches and strains some of us to prepare for greater weight in the future, during which we will have to not only carry our own burdens, but quite possibly the burdens of others. Thus our peace enables us to impart peace to others as we: "Bear one another's burdens, and so fulfill the law of Christ" (Galatians 6:2). And, if we truly become burden-bearing comforters, there is another product of peace to uplift us for "...counselors of peace have joy" (Proverbs 12:20b).

Hopefully, you can see peace is not an end in itself, for it brings with it many dividends in our own lives and the responsibility and opportunity to impart peace (both with and of God) to other hurting hearts. This peace is multiplied as each of us follow "the path of peace", and with watchful eyes, invite others to walk this same path with us to find God's peace to meet their every need. What joy to be able to share with others and to see them come to the place of peace and comfort which allows them to begin to reach out to others in "the Wonderful Exchange". That is my prayer for this book: I help you; you help them; and they help others. Is it any wonder those who work for the good of others, study about and do things which make for peace, will have the very comfort it brings? For truly "Blessed are the peacemakers" (Matthew 5:9a). We shall discuss more about peacemaking in chapter 12.

CHAPTER 8

THE ENEMIES OF PEACE

Now that we have found the way to bring peace into our lives and possibly have even begun to share this with others, we need to realize and explore a definite reality. That sad reality is there are dreadful and subtle enemies lurking both inside of and outside of our lives waiting to rob us of and destroy our peace. We may at first be tempted to blame Satan for this reality, and he can be partly to blame. However, the sad fact is most of the damage done to our peace is from self-inflicted wounds.

Even though we will be looking at several specific enemies of peace, I want to make it very clear from the beginning SIN DESTROYS PEACE. You will see each enemy is nothing more than a category of sin and therefore, a matter of willful choice on our part which will underscore the idea that the damage to our peace is self-inflicted. Whether we call it evil, iniquity, wickedness, disobedience, rebellion, the old nature, or just plain sin, the result is the same - separation from God. This separation, or enmity cuts us off from the source of peace, thereby stopping its flow to us. If we are unsaved, peace definitely cannot flow in our direction. If we are saved and we engage in sin, the flow is interrupted.

"But your iniquities have separated you from your God;
And your sins have hidden His face from you, So that
He will not hear." (Isaiah 59:2)

The sinner is separated, cut off from God and from the flow of His "peace like a river". Peace for today, and if unsaved for all eternity, is removed because of our own sin. What a sad comment on our inner desires; to choose sin over peace.

> "But the wicked are like the troubled sea, When it
> cannot rest, Whose waters cast up mire and dirt.
> **"There is no peace,"** Says my God, **"for the wicked."**
> (Isaiah 57:20-21 emphasis mine)

So listen as God describes the plight of sinful man:

> "The way of peace they have not known, And there is
> no justice in their ways; **They have made** themselves
> crooked paths; Whoever takes that way shall not know
> peace." (Isaiah 59:8, emphasis mine)

Notice "they made the crooked paths", a self-inflicted, self-chosen departure from "the path of peace." That is what sin (iniquity, wickedness, etc.) does for the person who chooses this path. It brings no peace, only things which will destroy peace and result in a very unsettled life for:

> "tribulation and anguish, on every soul of man who
> does evil…" (Romans 2:9a)

Because of the uncertainty of the future and the uneasiness of the present, the wicked also succumb to fear - fear of the unknown, fear of death, fear of judgment, fear of ruin, fear, fear, fear. Certainly, no peace where fear dominates.

> "There they are in great fear Where no fear was…
> Because God has despised them." (Psalm 53:5)

Sin in all its forms has a very disquieting effect on the soul. It also has its effects on our physical bodies and spirits as well. When David viewed his sin, he explained the many ways it disturbed not just his peace, but his entire being.

> "There is no soundness in my flesh Because of Your
> anger, Nor any health in my bones Because of my sin…
> For my iniquities have gone over my head; Like a
> heavy burden they are too heavy for me. ...
> I am troubled, I am bowed down greatly; I go mourning
> all the day long. ...
> I am feeble and severely broken; I groan because of the
> turmoil of my heart. ...
> My heart pants, my strength fails me; As for the light of
> my eyes, it also has gone from me." (Psalm 38:3a, 4, 6, 8, 10a)

The only remedies David could find were just as God had explained in His Word: confession and repentance.

> For I will declare my iniquity; I will be in anguish over my sin.
> (Psalm 38:18)

Not only does sin have its emotional effects on us, but it affects our vision as well. It is not our physical eyes and our sense of sight, but it is our spiritual sight that gets disturbed, keeping us from looking to the real source of peace - "the person of peace."

> For innumerable evils have surrounded me; My iniquities have
> overtaken me, so that **I am not able to look up**; They are more
> than the hairs of my head; Therefore my heart fails me.
> (Psalm 40:12, emphasis mine)

So, being unable to look up even brings fear causing the heart to fail. Certainly not a prescription for peace.

Our sin also stops our ears, disrupting our hearing. And yet, remember one of the keys to finding peace is hearing God's Word. We begin to turn a deaf ear to God when sin disrupts the communication channel, thus becoming much like static on a radio. We soon tire of the noise and either change the station or turn it off altogether. As you will see it also disrupts our prayer life.

> One who turns away his ear from hearing the law, Even his
> prayer is an abomination. (Proverbs 28:9)

In reality, static is some sort of interference, some problem between the source and the receiver. Sin is definitely spiritual static; it comes between us and God; a situation we described earlier as being at enmity with God "because the carnal (sinful) mind is enmity with God" (Romans 8:7).

If one is not careful and allows sin to completely destroy the river of peace flowing from God to man, it can have disastrous effects on even the memory of what peace was like.

> You have moved my soul far from peace; I have forgotten
> prosperity. (Lamentations 3:17)

Sin, as always, is a destructive force. It turns "peace like a river" into a disastrous torrent and flood of seemingly uncontrollable thoughts, emotions, and actions which bring trouble and trial into one's life. Small wonder God proclaims "the way of transgressors is hard" (Proverbs 13:15).

PRIDE

Ever since Satan uttered his five "I wills" (Isaiah 14:13-14), pride has been a problem. For mankind, it began as a problem right at the beginning in the garden of Eden when Adam and Eve decided "we will" do what we want, rather than what God had commanded (Genesis

3:6). In view of this, it should not surprise you that I view pride as the root of all sin. What else explains sin better, than it comes from our decision to do what "we will" rather than to follow God. Therefore, is it an enemy of peace?

Pride is sin, and we have already seen in general it has a great negative effect on our ability to find peace in this world. But what about pride specifically, does it bring specific negative consequences to our search for peace? Remember one of the first steps on "the path of peace" was "staying" our minds upon God. Well, pride certainly interferes with the desire and ability to do that, for we become gods to ourselves.

The wicked in his proud countenance does not seek God;
God is in none of his thoughts. (Psalm 10:4)

Because of pride, people have a secret (or open) wish to have no form of dependence upon God. They do not wish to be beholden to Him because their pride makes them feel they have no need of Him, they feel sufficient in themselves. What dangerous thinking. God must deal with such a heart attitude, not with peace, but with judgment. Ultimately, God will bring down the proud through repentance or ruin for:

Pride goes before destruction, And a haughty spirit before a fall.
(Proverbs 16:18)

Another of the many consequences of the proud heart is shame - not peace.

When pride comes, then comes shame… (Proverbs 11:2a)

God seems to be saying the one who exalts himself will be abased and contempt will be put upon him. Pride is a sin which brings shame to one's self and brings shame and disdain from others who observe it. If you disagree, just think how you feel about the person who is always bragging about himself, always portraying he is better than everyone else.

I hope no one reading this has ever had a fight (verbally or otherwise) with any other people, but have you wondered why people fight? No need to wonder any longer, the answer is PRIDE.

By pride comes nothing but strife… (Proverbs 13:10a)

The original word strife in the KJV was "contention" which Mr. Webster defines as "the act of contending; strife, struggle, controversy, dispute, quarrel." All this from pride. Why? Because I am smarter than you; what I have to say or my opinions are more important than yours; I AM ALWAYS RIGHT! Pride will sow discord and make men feel important and impatient. Men will be revenged and will not forgive because they are proud. You may have noticed a proud man is never wrong, and even when he is, he does not admit it. It is sort of like a sign my sister bought me which sits on one of my office shelves and reads "I could argue with you, but then we both would be wrong." Thus, the proud heart will find a way to save face and still appear to be more right than you or at least less wrong. It is easy to see pride of this sort does not lead to peace.

In his definition of contention, Mr. Webster used the same word the NKJV uses, the word "strife" His definition of this word adds depth to the consequences of pride by adding "the act of fighting or quarreling, esp. bitterly." Pride is definitely not a peacemaker. "Is too; is not; is too; is not; but my father is bigger than your father." Sounds like children, doesn't it? That is just the kind of bickering which comes from a proud heart for:

He who is of a proud heart stirs up strife… (Proverbs 28: 25a)

And, when you combine contention and strife, there is always trouble, not peace. All because of the pride of man's heart.

The beginning of strife is like releasing water; Therefore
stop contention before a quarrel starts. (Proverbs 17:14)

Contention and strife are like the proverbial snowball rushing
downhill, gathering speed and volume until it becomes almost
unstoppable, an avalanche if you will. We see in the verse above it is
likened to water as it begins to flow over the top of a dam. If like me, you
ever played "construction" as a child, you probably built a dam and then
watched as water began to fill it. Then with no place to go it spilled over
the top, breaching the top with an ever-increasing gap until the dam
literally broke, completely consumed by the force of the water. So it is
with strife and contentions; one word leads to another, and another, etc.,
until tempers flare beyond control. Tempers fueled by pride because I
am right and you think you are right. No small wonder God cautions
us to "stop" before trouble begins.

Thus, pride can never bring peace, but literally helps destroy it in our
lives and in the lives of others around us because of the shame, strife,
and contention it brings. No wonder that:

A man's pride will bring him low... (Proverbs 29:23)

Those who lift themselves up, talk big, are impressed with their
own importance, applaud themselves, bicker, and quarrel, will expose
themselves to the contempt of others. This pride, therefore, does not
bring peace from God but provokes God to bring them low.

Before leaving this subject of pride, allow me one last observation.
Pride in its pure essence is selfishness, and in truth, a selfish person is
never satisfied. I want what I want and I want it now. Only to find it is
not enough. Hardly a prescription for peace.

ANGER/WRATH/BITTERNESS/ETC.

There is a curious verse of Scripture that says: "Be angry, and do
not sin; do not let the sun go down on your wrath" (Ephesians 4:26). It

would appear then that prideful anger very easily becomes sin. Could it be anger and its cohorts, like the snowball rolling down the hill, can destroy peace? Most definitely! Anger, left to brood, leads in a downward spiral to less peaceful and peace-destroying emotions. Consider the following definitions (Webster) of anger and associated emotions.

Anger - a feeling of displeasure resulting from injury, maltreatment, opposition, etc., and usually showing itself in a desire to fight back at the supposed cause of the feeling. (Understand the "injustice" suffered may be real or simply perceived).

Bitterness - strong feelings of hatred, resentment, cynicism.

Hate - to have strong dislike or ill-will for, loathe; despise.

Malice - active ill-will; desire to harm another or to do mischief; spite.

Wrath - intense anger, rage; fury.

Revenge - to inflict pain or punishment because of; exact retribution for; avenge.

Note the definite increase in the intensity of the emotions and the propensity moving closer and closer to action against others. Certainly, anger is not on "the path of peace." If you think of it, the basic reason stems from the fact that an angry person thinks only of him/herself, which precludes him/her from "staying" their mind upon God. Thus, Solomon warns:

> Do not hasten in your spirit to be angry, For anger rests in the bosom of fools. (Ecclesiastes 7:9)

This verse explains two reasons why anger is not very compatible with peace. First, it is usually born out of a sense of selfish disappointment when instant gratification does not happen. Second, when in a selfish mood, one cannot stay his mind on God as already noted. Why?

Because the verse says he is a "fool" and "the fool has said in his heart, there is no God" (Psalm 14:1a).

So, if anger is not capable of producing peace, what does it do? An angry man stirs up strife, And a furious man abounds in transgression. (Proverbs 29:22)

A passionate, furious disposition flows from the man of pride bound by anger. People provoke one another and become provoking to one another, Also, one so wedded to his passions abounds in transgressions (SINS). This is not only because undue anger is sin, but anger also causes many other sins as it broods and broods and then erupts in sinful action. It stirs up trouble and increases in intensity as

Hatred stirs up strife… (Proverbs 10:12a)

See again the progression from bad to worse. Hatred is a great mischief-maker which blows on the dormant sparks of contention to fan it into a full-blown flame of passion. It would appear to even be on the prowl, looking for opportunities to wax worse possibly hoping "a harsh word stirs up anger"(Proverbs 15:1b). See how the flame grows and grows? I get angry (and blame you for making me that way); I retaliate; you get angry (and blame me); you retaliate; and on and on the vicious cycle goes. We quarrel thereby disturbing our peace, and when resentment is carried too far, one quarrel begets another. It is no small wonder "a wrathful man stirs up strife" (Proverbs 15:18a).

No my friend, anger does not bring peace, only heaviness to the soul; for those who do not have command of their emotions soon sink under the weight of them. This is not only an emotional weight, but also the load of our subsequent actions as anger left unchecked leads to cruel and outrageous acts.

A stone is heavy and sand is weighty, But a fool's wrath is
heavier than both of them. Wrath is cruel and anger a torrent...
(Proverbs 27:3, 4a)

Anger is much like throwing a small pebble into a large pond, the
ripples soon affect the whole surface. A small impact, yet it grows and
grows in its influence on an ever-widening circle of people. The anger
begins to spill over onto innocent people who are guilty of simply
being by-standers. No wonder the writer of Hebrews gives us the
following caution:

Looking carefully lest anyone fall short of the grace of God;
lest any root of bitterness springing up cause trouble, and by this
many become defiled. (Hebrews 12:15)

There is the product of anger; it is the "bitter root". One does not
have to be a farmer or horticulturist to know a bitter root produces
bitter fruit. Anyone who has tasted something bitter knows that if we
hand it to someone else, it will be bitter to them as well. Thus, self or
others, it matters not, for only bitterness can result. Anger brings bad
principles and bad habits, which defile self and those around us.

Think back to the last time you tasted something really bitter. What
was your reaction? If you are like me, you probably spit it out as quickly
as possible and complained about the taste with a loud "blah, yuk". See
again the cycle which anger brings. Anger brings bitterness; bitterness
brings bitter fruit (like more internal anger or an angry reaction from
another); and bitter fruit brings complaining. Could this be the reason
why Job said "I will speak in the anguish of my spirit; I will complain
in the bitterness of my soul" (Job 7:11b). Could this be why God
admonishes us to:

Cease from anger, and forsake wrath; Do not fret-
it only causes harm. (Psalm 37:8)

and to:

> Let all bitterness, wrath, anger, clamor, and evil speaking
> be put away from you, with all malice. (Ephesians 4:31)

I can sum this section up with a quote I just read online from Andy Rooney. "When you harbor bitterness, happiness (and peace) will dock elsewhere" (insertion mine).

DEPRESSION

Whether depression brings lack of peace or lack of peace brings depression is sort of like "which came first, the chicken or the egg" debate. Suffice it to say, they are inseparable. As a counselor, I do know a major fruit of internalized anger is depression - another side effect of the previous section. That's right, depression consists largely of anger turned inward upon one's self. Other possible components are self-pity and hopelessness. Again, what goes on in the mind affects the very heart and soul much as a tree bends with the direction of the wind. Listen as the writer of Proverbs describes the unmerciful condition of depression:

> Anxiety in the heart of man causes depression…
> (Proverbs 12:25a)

The original KJV translated the word anxiety as heaviness, but either word conveys the idea they can be either the cause of or the consequence of a depressed emotional state. One who carries a load of anger, care, fear, sorrow, etc. puts a heavy burden upon his spirit thus causing depression or in the KJV to cause it to "stoop". Picture one stooped over with a heavy burden, and you will realize how the weight of the burden makes them sink under the load and be even more weighed down with care.

When one is so burdened and stooped over, it is hard to look up and find any solution to the perplexing problems which so easily besiege the soul. No wonder hopelessness comes on the heels of low-down feelings. It seems there is nothing more grievous than the disappointment of a raised expectation never fulfilled. It simply kills the heart, for "hope deferred makes the heart sick..." (Proverbs 13:12a). But my dear friend, don't lose hope for: *The LORD upholds all who fall, And raises up all who are bowed down* (Psalm 145:14).

We need to also note that left unchecked, depression not only affects emotional peace, but may have physical consequences as well. The sorrows of the mind often contribute much to the sickness of the body, as Solomon had in mind when he said "...a broken spirit dries the bones" (Proverbs 17:22b). This could be illustrated by the picture of an old-fashioned three-legged milk stool. Try sitting on one of these with one leg broken. It is almost impossible, especially if you were going to try to do some milking. We humans were created by God as three-legged or rather three-part (tripartite) beings - body, soul, and spirit. If there is a problem in one part of the body long enough, it eventually will affect the other parts. For example, if we are sick (body) long enough, the soul (mental/emotional) and spirit begin to have problems. If we have mental/emotional problems too long, the body becomes affected. God's answer to restore body, soul, and spirit is to be "casting all your care upon Him, for He cares for you"(I Peter 5:7) as we addressed in chapter six.

WORRY

One of the greatest hindrances to peace I am aware of is the fruitless human endeavor known as "worry". It is a peace-breaker like few others in its widespread infection of the entirety of mankind. Worry, worry, worry, wring your hands, and worry some more. What a plague! Interestingly enough is the fact that most people are almost proud of being worriers. They will readily admit they are worriers, even come from a family of worriers.

I do need to address the word "fruitless" from the first sentence. It is fruitless in the sense that worry never fixed anything, never came up with a solution. I was challenging a man about his worry one day in my office when he slammed his fist down on my desk and said, "Don't' tell me worry doesn't work!" When I asked him why he thought it worked, he again slammed his fist down and said, "Nothing I ever worried about ever happened." Hopefully over the next few minutes I convinced him he had spent a lot of time and mental/emotional effort on things which never happened. However, it is also fruitful in the sense that it bears the bad fruits of things like anxiety and depression. And, dear friend, remember **worry is sin**, and as does all sin, detracts from our ability to find peace.

If you were to hear me speak on the topic of worry, one of the reasons I would stress as to the sinfulness of worry is because it is a lack of faith, and "whatever is not from faith is sin" (Romans 14:23b). Think back with me to the story found in Mark 4 when the disciples were afraid of the storm-tossed sea. Christ had said "Let us cross over to the other side" (vs. 35), and yet, as the wind blew and the waves rose, the disciples began to worry even though they were in the very presence of God Himself. After calming the storm with these simple words, "Peace, be still!" (vs. 39), Christ rebukes them in the form of two questions: "Why are you so fearful? How is it that you have no faith?" (vs. 40)

Is it any wonder God admonishes us to "Be anxious for nothing" (Philippians 4:6)? He is plainly saying "do not worry". We are also given this same message in other ways such as "fret not". Consider another verse which clearly points out the effect worry has on today.

Therefore do not worry about tomorrow, for tomorrow
will worry about its own things. Sufficient for the day is
its own trouble. (Matthew 6:34)

The word "trouble" in the Greek denotes evil, adversity, and/or misfortune. All of those would make today bad enough, but we insist on burdening today by worrying about tomorrow which is not even here yet. Then if we are not careful, we can further rob today of its peace by bringing yesterday into the picture as well. The following illustration should show how worry and other enemies of peace can make today a "less than peaceful" event.

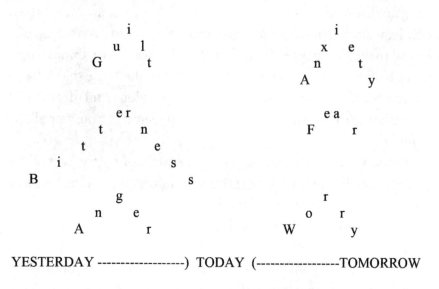

YESTERDAY ------------------) TODAY (-----------------TOMORROW

We could add all sorts of other components to the above diagram which would fill our day with care (greed, envy, jealousy, etc.), which we will consider later in this chapter. After all, these things fill the mind and make it impossible to "stay our minds upon God". Thus, peace ceases to exist as "the enemies of peace" erode away the blessings and joy of today. As to the past, the French philosopher Voltaire commented, "The longer we dwell on our misfortunes, the greater is their power to harm us." Senator Bill Bradley put it this way: "…the more you carry the past around, the less likely it is that the future will improve." As to the present and future, a secular song of not long ago put it, "Don't worry, be happy."

If you want to restore peace to yesterday, then the solution is probably forgiveness or in releasing the problem to God. You can't change it anyhow so why let it control today? To assure today's and tomorrow's peace, there is faith in God and his promises. As the following saying indicates, peace comes from living in the present.

Yesterday is history
Tomorrow is a mystery;
Today is a gift, that is
why is it called the "present".

Or, as another old saying goes:

Sorrow looks back;
Worry looks around;
Faith looks up!

Catch that! Faith looks up where it can be "stayed upon Jehovah" where it can find peace, "for to be spiritually minded is life and peace"(Romans 8:6b) .

GREED

Webster defines greed as: "excessive desire for getting or having, especially wealth; desire for more than one needs or deserves; avarice, cupidity." Along those lines, I once read a statement by one of the billionaire Rockefellers in response to a question as to how much money it would take to satisfy him. His answer: "One more dollar!" That should make it easy to understand how greed destroys peace as the mind fills with a lust for things, and thus crowds out God so He cannot be "stayed upon."

…thou hast greedily gained of thy neighbors
by extortion, and **hast forgotten me**, saith the
Lord God. (Ezekiel 22:12 KJV, emphasis mine)

If we forget God, if we no longer stay our minds upon Him, is there any choice but to concentrate on our own wishes, fantasies, hopes and dreams? Look as Isaiah describes the condition of the greedy:

Yes, they are greedy dogs Which never have enough.
And they are shepherds Who cannot understand; They all **look to
their own way,** Every one for his own gain, From his own territory.
(Isaiah 56:11, emphasis mine)

Notice how those consumed by greed can never have enough, are
never satisfied, cannot understand, and look to their own way. These
are the tragic consequences from pulling their minds away from God
onto the things of this world. They will never have enough; they will
never be satisfied; they will always need (want) more, for

He who loves silver will not be satisfied with silver; Nor
he who loves abundance, with increase. This also is vanity.
(Ecclesiastes 5:10)

They cannot understand because
A man's steps are of the LORD; How then can a man
understand his own way? (Proverbs 20:24)

If people cannot understand, how can they even then begin to look
to their own way? Our own way! Minding one's own way means that
our own private interests are of the utmost importance with no thought
of the welfare of others. Sounds like the essence of pride - another
enemy of peace. Greed for our own way causes us to look to self and
away from God.

For all seek their own, not the things which are of
Christ Jesus. (Philippians 2:21)

Is it any wonder when we consider the greed of mankind that :
The LORD looks down from heaven upon the children
of men, To see if there are any who understand, who
seek God. (Psalm 14:2)

And we find the result in verse 3, He found "no, not one".

Greed is one of those sins which can soon sear a conscience and result in dreadful acts which have nothing to do with peace, except as peace is sought out in material gain or physical pleasure. Listen as Paul describes such people.

> Who, being past feeling, have given themselves over
> to lewdness, to work all uncleanness with greediness.
> (Ephesians 4:19)

These are not peaceful people; they are past feeling with consciences seared. They have no sense of their sin, nor of the danger and misery of their situation because of it. They have yielded themselves to every lust and have committed all sorts of uncleanness with insatiable desires (greed) controlling their lives. When men so set their hearts on their own satisfaction, when their consciences are seared, there are no boundaries to their sin, and sin destroys peace. Plainly put, if I am never satisfied, I am never at peace.

Like all sin, the consequences are not self-contained, they often affect those around us, especially our families. So it is with greed for "he who is greedy for gain troubles his own house" (Proverbs 15:27a) Greed makes one a slave to material things and brings trouble to the family of the greed-controlled person as he worries and frets at every loss and disappointment. Greed also causes one to quarrel with anybody and everybody who stands in the way of his profit. Certainly, greed does not make for peace.

GREEN-EYED MONSTERS

Relatives to greed are the "green-eyed monster" sins of jealousy, covetousness, and envy, which stand on the ramparts as definite enemies of peace. Each has at the center of its "eye" a root of selfishness - sin. Yet they are different, and we need to consider their definitions (Webster) and look to the Word of God to see their impact on the pursuit of peace.

JEALOUSY - the quality or condition of being jealous - i.e. resentfully suspicious of a rival or a rival's influence.

Suspicion and selfishness are certainly not precursors to peace; and when resentful they are more likely precursors to anger as Solomon found in Proverbs 6:34 when he stated, "For jealousy is a husband's fury; Therefore he will not spare in the day of vengeance." He went on to explain the consequences of jealousy in his treatise on love known as the Song of Solomon.

> ...Jealousy is cruel as the grave; Its flames are flames of
> fire, A most vehement flame. (Song of Solomon 8:6b)

The word "grave" used here refers to the grave that swallows up and devours all. Compare that to the analogy of "flames of fire" which also devours everything in its path. Thus, we have an accurate portrait of the destructive (not peaceful) force of this monster we call jealousy.

COVETOUSNESS - the act of wanting ardently (especially something that another person has); long for with envy.

> Is it any wonder why God would simply admonish us that:
> You shall not covet your neighbor's house; you shall not
> covet your neighbor's wife, nor his male servant, nor his
> female servant, nor his ox, nor his donkey, nor anything
> that is your neighbor's. (Exodus 20:17)

When we consider the effect "wanting" can have on our personal peace, we begin to understand how "wants" turn into perceived "needs" and the sense of urgency to acquire things grows and grows. There seems to be something about "wanting" out of covetousness which brings thoughts of discontent with our own lot and ends with envy of our neighbor's lot. Neither covetousness nor envy produce or are conducive to an atmosphere of peace. The writer of Hebrews echoes this idea and shows how contentment and God's faithfulness are reasons why covetousness and envy are not necessary.

> Let your conduct be without covetousness; be content
> with such things as you have. For He Himself has said,
> "I will never leave you nor forsake you." (Hebrews 13:5)

This over-eager desire for the wealth and comfort of the world, this envying of those who have more than we, puts a wrong emphasis on life, for our happiness and comfort do not depend upon our having a great deal of wealth. The apostle Luke bears this out when he states:

> Take heed and beware of covetousness, for one's life
> does not consist in the abundance of the things he
> possesses. (Luke 12:15)

It appears Luke is telling us the things of this world will not suit the nature of the soul, nor supply its needs, or satisfy its desires, or last as long as the soul will last. The pursuit of "things" is simply frustrating at best, for there is never enough to satisfy. Even should we come to the point when we feel we have "enough", there is then the burden of caring for it and protecting it. Then there may be guilt for the way we acquired it, and the time and trouble with counting, saving, and using it. This doesn't sound peaceful, does it? In fact, Habakkuk pronounced a "woe" upon this "wanting" which we know as covetousness.

> Woe to him who covets evil gain for his house, That he
> may set his nest on high, That he may be delivered from
> the power of disaster! (Habakkuk 2:9)

"Woe" for coveting; "woe" for coveting "more", as one caught in the trap of this peace-destroyer wants ever more and more, aiming even higher and higher. This is especially an evil thing in a family. It brings disquiet and uneasiness into the home as "he who is greedy for gain troubles his own house..." (Proverbs 15:27). Listen as the Apostle Paul reveals the results of coveting especially as applied to "money":

> For the love of money is a root of all kinds of evil, for
> which some have strayed from the faith in their greediness,
> and pierced themselves through with many sorrows.
> (I Timothy 6:10)

Wait! Because of greed there are all kinds of evil, they stray from the faith, and pierce themselves with many sorrows. No peace there, even with all they have acquired.

God's prescription for peace in this area of life is found two verses earlier.

> And having food and clothing, with these we shall be
> content. (I Timothy 6:8)

And, if we would believe the wisdom of Solomon, this matter of covetousness could be laid to rest for:

> ..he who hates covetousness will prolong his days.
> (Proverbs 28:16b"

The last of the "green-eyed monsters" is envy. Listen as Mr. Webster defines this peace-breaker:

ENVY - a feeling of discontent and ill-will because of another's advantages, possessions, etc.; resentful dislike of another who has something that one desires.

Just reading this definition brings a sense of uneasiness with words such as "discontent", "ill-will" and "resentful dislike". None of these are conducive to peace. Listen as the writer of Proverbs gives Biblical insight as to the personal destructiveness of envy:

> Wrath is cruel, and anger is outrageous, but who
> is able to stand before envy? (Proverbs 27:4 KJV)

The idea here seems to be that envy becomes a pursuer. It goes from wanting something another has, to an enmity against the person themselves, then on to anger, then to a desire to hurt, thus leaving the envious stuck in the cycle of his envy. Following this path leads not only to emotional problems, but physical as well.

> A sound heart is life to the body, But envy is rottenness to
> the bones. (Proverbs 14:30

This verse well indicates how much our health, our very "peace" depends on the control of and proper use of our "passions" and the maintenance of an even temper of mind. A fretful, envious, discontented spirit is its own worst enemy and becomes its own punishment. It consumes the flesh, preys upon the human spirit, makes the countenance pale, and is truly the "rottenness" of the bones. Those who see the prosperity of others and are envious and thus grieved will:

> The wicked will see it and be grieved; He will gnash his
> teeth and melt away; The desire of the wicked shall perish.
> (Psalm 112:10)

The writer of James gives us the true results of envy, which do not include anything approximating peace.

> For where envy and self-seeking exist, confusion and
> every evil thing are there. (James 3:16)

By now you should see this green-eyed monster is not a one-eyed Cyclops; it is an ugly three-eyed creature whose sole purpose is to rob us of our peace with its jealousy, covetousness, and envy. These three work their poison in the heart and destroy peace from the inside. If we want peace, we need to be careful of what we desire:

"For where your treasure is, there your heart will be also.
(Matthew 6:21)

FEAR

Mr. Webster defined fear as: "apprehension of evil or danger; dread; anxiety". Just think back to a time when you were scared - afraid. Was that a peaceful feeling? Was your mind "stayed" upon God?

To illustrate why the emotion of fear is not a producer of peace, we need only to look at a story of one of the Old Testament men of God to find how fear robs one of peace. In Genesis 31 and verse 3 God commands Jacob to "return to the land of his fathers", and then presents him with a promise that "I will be with thee". In chapter 32 verse 9 we find God meant "I will deal well with you" because of His presence, His power, and His protection. Yet in verse 7 of chapter 32 as Jacob hears that his brother Esau is coming to meet him, "Jacob was greatly afraid and distressed".

Why would he become afraid? Hadn't God promised it would be "well" for Jacob? You have probably figured it out for yourself, but the answer is that like worry, fear is a lack of faith in God's promise and, therefore, is sin; and SIN DESTROYS PEACE. It destroys peace because of its lack of faith, but it also destroys peace as it controls the mind with fearful (not peaceful) thoughts. In fact, fear becomes a trap with a definite enticement to sin. As Solomon put it:

The fear of man brings a snare, But whoever trusts
in the LORD shall be safe. (Proverbs 29:25)

There are many stories told by trappers of how a wolf or fox chewed off its own leg to be freed from a trap. Sounds like a very desperate measure, doesn't it? Yet this is how the trap of fear works; it brings desperate acts of sin to be freed from the mental anguish stirred within the breast. Fear leads to the sin of lack of faith "for whatever is not of faith is sin" (Romans 14:23b). It may lead to sin as fear of the world (peer pressure), or fear of someone more powerful in strength or authority causes us to succumb to temptation, or to simply bow in sin. And yet God says to us, much as He did to Jacob, "Fear not, for I am with you" (Isaiah: 43:5a). God in this promise does not leave us in a vulnerable position all alone, for the true promise of God for His children puts our situation, our peace, solely in the providence of His care.

Fear not, for I am with you; Be not dismayed, for I am your God. I will strengthen you, Yes, I will help you, I will uphold you with My righteous right hand.
(Isaiah 41:10)

Compare this to the New Testament promise for God's children given to young Timothy by the Apostle Paul.

For God has not given us a spirit of fear, but of power and of love and of a sound mind. (II Timothy 1:7)

A sound mind "sounds" peaceful, and it is attainable by "staying our minds", not just on the promise, but on the faithfulness of the Promisor. There's the rub - fear takes our minds off almighty God and thereby destroys peace. King David found this correlation to be true and recorded it for us in Psalm 63:

The path - staying our mind on God.
When I remember You on my bed, I meditate on You in the night watches. (Psalm 63:6)

The result - peace.
My soul shall be satisfied as with marrow and fatness,
And my mouth shall praise You with joyful lips.
(Psalm 63:5)

Or, as Solomon found:

When you lie down, you will not be afraid; Yes, you
will lie down and your sleep will be sweet.
(Proverbs 3:24)

For David, the solution to fear was simple. "When I am afraid, I will trust in you" (Psalm 56:3). A simple return to the foundation of peace - a mind stayed upon God. And, check this out, if you don't believe God has ways of His mysterious wonders to perform. Yesterday I had lunch after church in a Chinese restaurant and here is what my fortune cookie told me:

"Fear knocked on the door. Faith answered. No one was there."

GUILT

One of the other mental/emotional things which seems to sap peace from a life is guilt. The particular definition from Mr. Webster which applies here says: "A painful feeling of self-reproach resulting from a belief that one has done something wrong or immoral." See the concentration again on SELF and away from "staying on God". Joseph's brothers, who had sold him into slavery, felt this guilt in a very real way.

Then they said to one another, "We are truly guilty
concerning our brother, for we saw the anguish of his
soul when he pleaded with us, and we would not hear;
therefore this distress has come upon us.
(Genesis 42:21)

This feeling we call guilt comes basically in two forms - real and false, both of which have a great propensity for destroying peace.

Real guilt occurs when we break a law or standard, be it man's or God's. Exceed the speed limit, guilty of speeding; tell a lie, guilty of lying. This type of guilt does not necessarily carry with it a lot of feeling (until the flashing red lights go off in your rear- view mirror). However, there is an easy antidote (confession) to insure its effect on peace is short-lived. As we saw with the brothers of Joseph, time alone will not erase the staggering weight which guilt can bring to the mind and emotions; there must be confession The old saying "confession is good for the soul" certainly must have had Biblical roots because:

> If we confess our sins, he is faithful and just to forgive us our sins, and to cleanse us from all unrighteousness. (1 John 1:9)

We should probably note that "confession" is more than mere verbal assent that we have sinned; it is to agree with God about my sin, and God HATES sin. Therefore, if we agree with Him, then we will give it up, which not only re-establishes our peace but insures its continuance.

UNEQUAL YOKE

All of us know what happens when we put just one "bad" apple into the barrel - they all spoil. This happens to us as children of God whenever we link ourselves to the world, whether by friendship, marriage or business relationships. We all feel we can maintain our testimonies, stay away from sinful choices; but the sad fact is that normally we are drawn into sinful actions, and SIN DESTROYS PEACE. This is why God made very clear His desire when He commanded us to:

> Do not be unequally yoked together with unbelievers.
> For what fellowship has righteousness with lawlessness?
> And what communion has light with darkness?
> (II Corinthians 6:14)

If you don't believe this, just go to the book of Judges and other places in the Old Testament and see what happened to God's chosen people (Israel) when they continually got "yoked" to the cultures around them.

The Apostle Luke comments on how following God's directions can literally bring peace to us.

> But whatever house you enter, first say, "Peace to this house."' And if a son of peace is there, your peace will rest on it; if not, it will return to you.
> (Luke 10:5-6)

PRAYER

PRAYER??? I can almost see you sitting there with a deeply furrowed brow wondering how prayer can be an "enemy of peace". As I address this enemy, think about your own prayer life. Haven't you ever prayed and prayed and become frustrated. Frustrated because God didn't answer right away, frustrated because God didn't answer in the way you expected, frustrated because He didn't give you what you wanted. Frustration, impatience, wrong attitudes, etc, are examples of the types of things which can cause prayer to lead us away from rather than bring peace.

The fist consideration is: "To whom do you pray?" It must be to the one true God - Jehovah, the God of Abraham, Isaac, and Jacob, the Father of our Lord and Savior Jesus Christ. You see, to believe in and pray to "a" god is not enough. You must know the real God and know who He is. Again we can reference Israel when they succumbed to the cultures around them

> …They have no knowledge, Who carry the wood of their carved image, And pray to a god that cannot save.
> (Isaiah 45:20b)

If you remember, the first step on "the path of peace" is to obtain "peace with God". Thus, it is not only necessary to pray to the right God, but you must also know Him personally and be able to call Him Father, because:

> Now we know that God does not hear sinners; but if anyone is a worshiper of God and does His will, He hears him. (John 9:31)

It is my firm belief the first prayer that God hears from any of us is "God be merciful to me a sinner" (Luke 18:13b).

By now you hopefully agree praying to the wrong god, or praying to the true God without belonging to His family cannot possibly contribute to peace. But what about the Christian, how can prayer be an enemy to his peace? The answer is the same one word which describes all of the enemies of peace - SIN. Sin disrupts the communication link between God and us like static on a radio because:

> If I regard iniquity in my heart, The Lord will not hear.
> (Psalm 66:18)

If we are living in sin, loving it, indulging in it, allowing ourselves to be controlled by it, and if we have a light-hearted view of the sins of others, God does not hear us and will not answer our prayer. So, we pray, and pray in vain, and become impatient and frustrated, but we are not at peace. For only:

> The effective, fervent prayer of a righteous man avails much. (James 5:16b)

To repeat an earlier verse, the Apostle John combines the ideas of praying to the right God, personally knowing God, and lack of sin as seen in our obedience to Him when he says under the inspiration of the Holy Spirit:

> Now we know that God does not hear sinners; but if anyone is a worshiper of God and does His will, He hears him. (John 9:31)

Or, as King David stated:

> The righteous cry out, and the LORD hears, And delivers them out of all their troubles. (Psalm 34:17)

As with salvation, faith is the real key to prayer which gets answers and brings peace. Faith which is right brings forth prayer, but prayer is not right unless it springs from faith. Faith is the condition of receiving. No faith - no answer. No faith - no peace. Remember the wicked are like the storm-tossed sea. Listen to the description of the one who prays without faith.

> But let him ask in faith, with no doubting, for he who doubts is like a wave of the sea driven and tossed by the wind. For let not that man suppose that he will receive anything from the Lord. (James 1:6-7)

> On the contrary, the prayer of faith will be rewarded. And whatever things you ask in prayer, believing, you will receive. (Matthew 21:22)

Many of us can also make prayer a matter of frustration because we know what we want, and when we want it (NOW!). Or we pray in an attempt to dictate to God how and when He should do it. For instance, we all know God is not willing any should perish (II Peter 3:9), so in our prayer we presume to tell Him just what steps to take so that old so-and-so gets saved and to do it today. We need to remember, as did our Lord, to pray "Your will be done" (Luke 11:2). When we try to impose our will and our timetable upon the Almighty God, we are in for frustration, not peace. We need to remember that prayer, like the way we live our daily lives, must be according to God's will.

> For you have need of endurance, so that **after** you
> have done the will of God, you may receive the promise.
> (Hebrews 10:36, emphasis mine)

Another way in which prayer can be an "enemy of peace" is simply not to pray at all. To make the decisions of life without consulting God will certainly not contribute to "the path of peace". James puts it very simply by combining lack of obedience with lack of prayer as to how once again prayer can become frustrating, not peaceful:

> You lust and do not have. You murder and covet
> and cannot obtain. You fight and war. Yet you do
> not have because **you do not ask**.
> (James 4:2, emphasis mine)

In the very next verse James addresses another reason prayer can become an "enemy of peace".

> You ask and do not receive, because you ask amiss,
> that you may spend it on your pleasures (lust-KJV).
> (James 4:3, insertion mine)

Imagine people praying for something they lust after, something to bring them pleasure, praying literally that God would give them something they didn't need or was sinful, or praying to legitimize or excuse their sin. That type of prayer violates just about every principle we have mentioned. Small wonder this type of praying does not bring peace.

Allow me to illustrate how praying could become an "enemy of peace" with an example from my own life. I have already mentioned I was an avid fisherman, and I was an equally (maybe even more so) avid hunter. As a young lad while deer hunting, I remember standing on watch, stomping my cold feet, bowing my head, and praying something like, "Dear Heavenly Father, when I open my eyes let there be a huge buck standing there and let my bullet fly straight, In the name of Jesus, Amen." I would immediately look around and, you guessed it, there was no large buck standing there for me to shoot. Then I would tell myself that I knew God wouldn't answer my prayer (wavering faith), or, that it wasn't really God's will (my prayer was amiss to satisfy my own lusts outside of His will).

But, just suppose I had not understood the fallacy of my prayer? Had I felt I had prayed a fervent, faithful prayer, I might have become disillusioned with prayer, and maybe even God Himself. Thus, my friend, pray right, pray peacefully.

TONGUE

The next "enemy of peace" which I want to consider is not so much an emotional or mental state, as it is the part of our body most used in a sinful manner to contribute to the destruction of peace, brought on by the enemies we have already discussed. Old adages such as "the pen is mightier that the sword" point to the power of words, but in particular the power of the spoken word, for truly "the tongue is sharper that the sword". Is it any wonder we are cautioned to "think before speaking", or to "engage the brain before inserting foot"?

> Do you see a man hasty in his words? There is more
> hope for a fool than for him. (Proverbs 29:20)

Like no other part of the body, the tongue has great power and propensity for the destruction of peace. Listen as James sheds yet another scriptural perspective on the tongue.

> And the tongue is a fire, a world of iniquity. The tongue is so
> set among our members that it defiles the whole body, and sets
> on fire the course of nature; and it is set on fire by hell. For
> every kind of beast and bird, of reptile and creature of the sea,
> is tamed and has been tamed by mankind. But no man can tame the
> tongue. It is an unruly evil, full of deadly poison. (James 3:6-8)

In fact, the problems wrought by the tongue are so great that of the seven abominations unto God listed in Proverbs 6:16-19, three of them are matters of the tongue: a lying tongue, a false witness, and sowing discord among the brethren. Sin and the tongue appear to go together like birds of a feather. Wickedness begets a wicked tongue, and a wicked tongue fosters wickedness.

> Everyone will deceive his neighbor, And will not speak
> the truth; They have taught their tongue to speak lies;
> They weary themselves to commit iniquity. (Jeremiah 9:5)

As we think back over the "enemies of peace", see how the tongue can be used in each one to bring destruction (fire and poison) and hamper or destroy peace.

PRIDE - "I am", the root of even Satan's sin

ANGER/WRATH/BITTERNESS - "I hate you; I'm going to get even; I'm going to lie about you and get you into trouble" - cutting words from an angry heart.

DEPRESSION - "I am worthless, there is no hope, all is lost."

WORRY - constantly talking about that which brings anxiety, not allowing the mind to come to rest.

GREED- gimme, gimme. gimme. Or lying to get our heart's desire.

JEALOUSY/COVETOUSNESS/ENVY - sarcastic, cynical, cutting remarks, disparaging the "goods" of others. "I want"; "I wish I had".

FEAR - lying about our fear so as not to appear foolish in the eyes of others (linked to pride), crying out in fear and disturbing others..

GUILT - self-deprecating remarks or lying to get out of the situation.

UNEQUAL YOKE - flattery and self-talk (lying) to convince ourselves and others of the "rightness" of our yoke. "I can witness to them and lead them to the Lord." "It was God's will for us to be together."

Prayer - asking amiss to consume it upon our lust (greed/envy, etc.)

Then there is another SIN that the tongue can be involved in which is another definite enemy of peace - GOSSIP.

>...he who repeats a matter separates friends.
>(Proverbs 17:9b)

The Scriptures are very clear about how gossip is related to the destruction of peace.

>Where there is no wood, the fire goes out; And where there is no talebearer, strife ceases. As charcoal is to burning coals, and wood to fire, So is a contentious man to kindle strife. The words of a talebearer are like tasty trifles, And they go down into the inmost body. (Proverbs 26:20-22)

So "be careful little tongue what you say", if you want to have and to maintain your peace, for in the guarding of the tongue comes peace and long life.

> Whoever guards his mouth and tongue keeps his soul from troubles. (Proverbs 21:23)

> For He who would love life And see good days, Let him refrain his tongue from evil, And his lips from speaking deceit. (1 Peter 3:10)

UNBELEIF

Next, and probably one of the worst destroyers of peace is unbelief, simply not believing or trusting God when He says:

> And we know that all things work together for good to those who love God, to those who are the called according to His purpose. (Romans 8:28)

> No temptation has overtaken you except such as is common to man; but God is faithful, who will not allow you to be tempted beyond what you are able, but with the temptation will also make the way of escape, that you may be able to bear it. (I Corinthians 10:13)

> So, Jesus said to them, "Because of your unbelief; for assuredly, I say to you, if you have faith as a mustard seed, you will say to this mountain, 'Move from here to there,' and it will move; and nothing will be impossible for you. (Matthew 17:20)

Unbelief defiles our mind and conscience, it does nothing to bring peace.

To the pure all things are pure, but to those who are defiled and unbelieving nothing is pure; but even their mind and conscience are defiled. (Titus 1:15)

Unbelief makes sure we do not "stay our minds" on God, but to rather depart from Him.
Beware, brethren, lest there be in any of you an evil heart of unbelief in departing from the living God. (Hebrews 3:12)

It also hardens our heart, making peace so much more elusive.
…exhort one another daily, while it is called "Today," lest any of you be hardened through the deceitfulness of sin. (Hebrews 3:13)

And ultimately, unbelief keeps us from ever being at peace:

And to whom sware he that they should not enter into his rest, but to them that believed not? (Hebrews 3:18 KJV)

One other major factor of unbelief leading to all sin and lack of peace, is simply we do not believe Romans chapter 6 which clearly teaches we do not have to sin, that we could live sinless lives and have ultimate peace. Not possible you say, but why do you sin? You want to, you choose to, you don't have to. Look at what God says about the saint's relationship to sin.

vs. 6 Crucified with Him that we should not serve sin.
vs. 8 Freed from sin.
vs.11 Dead to sin.
vs. 14 Sin has no dominion over you.
vs. 18 Free from sin.
vs. 22 Free from sin.

Could it be any plainer? But we do not believe, we have made idols of our humanity, our sinful nature. We believe we are "only" human and have no power over sin and use our nature as an excuse for our sin, and "sin destroys peace". It seems like every time I broach this subject, the response I get is "we are only human". If that is true, then we do not even believe the Holy Spirit lives within us with all of the power of God at our disposal.

The Apostle Paul even struggled with this idea in Romans chapter 7 about the way our spirit and our flesh collide and fight for dominance. But he is the one God used to write chapter 6 and then to sum it up in chapter 8 thusly:

For the law of **the Spirit of life in Christ Jesus has made me free** from the law of sin and death. (Romans 8:2, emphasis mine)

Since all of the enemies of peace are sin, sin, and more sin, you may feel there is no solution, no victory to be had, no peace for us to claim. Be at peace dear friend, God has provided a path for dealing with all sin problems that hinder our peace. That path is called "confession".

If we confess our sins, He is faithful and just to forgive us our sins and to cleanse us from all unrighteousness. (1 John 1:9)

This step restores our peace "of" God which had been disrupted by our sin. However, I would provide one note of caution regarding the true meaning on the word "confession" in this verse. This is not a mere verbal assent that "I have sinned". The word literally means to "agree with God about my sin", and God HATES sin. Thus, you can see it means a true repentant attitude and change of heart.

Stated simply, "Sin destroys peace, salvation brings peace; sin destroys peace, repentant confession restores peace".

NEGATIVISM

Lastly, I believe there is one huge human propensity which destroys our peace, and I put it this way: "Because of our sinful nature, we are negatively charged". By that I mean, we are so **prone** to focus on the negative that we can become so **focused** on the negative we become **consumed** by it. Let me illustrate the point this way. Look at the space below and tell yourself what you see.

●

If you are like hundreds of people I have done this with, you saw the black dot. But wait, didn't you ignore all the white space which is more than 99.9% of the area. Think about how much a little negative issue can get "under your skin" and completely captivate your thinking pattern - leading to worry, anxiety, anger, etc.

I had a woman come for a marriage counseling session, and she proceeded to let me know just how bad her husband was. My response shocked her as I said, "You have the worst husband I have ever heard of!" She wanted to know where I had gotten such an idea. "From you!" As we talked, I asked her if he was 100%, 90% bad, and as I worked her all the way down to 5% her answer was always "No". So, I asked her about a couple of the specific details from years ago. She could give the date, time and what he was wearing. How could she do that? She could do that because she had spent years focusing on those black dots. I knew her husband had accepted Christ as his Savior about five years earlier and asked her to give me similar black dots since then - with a recognition of shame she realized she could not. Removing the black dots not only improved her marriage but restored peace to her heart.

All of this points to what God said in Proverbs 23:7: "For as he thinketh in his heart, so is he" (KJV). That thought is captured by the following statement:

Your life is a reflection of your thoughts.
If you change your thinking, you change your life.

That agrees with what the Apostle Paul says in Philippians 4:5-9 where he lays out God's prescription for the "peace that passes all understanding". Prayer and thinking about good things are God's simple solution. Why do we make it so hard?

Let me close this idea by repeating a similar version of a story from chapter 7 which I found illustrating the black dot and the solution so very well.

The only survivor of a shipwreck was washed up on a small uninhabited island. He prayed feverishly for God to rescue him and every day he scanned the horizon for help, but none seemed forthcoming.

Exhausted, he eventually managed to build a little hut out of driftwood to protect himself from the elements, and to store his few possessions. But then one day, after scavenging for food, he arrived home to find his little hut in flames, the smoke rolling up into the sky. The worst had happened; everything was lost. He was stunned with grief and anger. "God, how could you do this to me" he cried.

Early the next day, however, he was awakened by the sound of a ship that was approaching the island. It had come to rescue him. "How did you know I was here?" asked the weary man of his rescuers. "We saw your smoke signal", they replied.

It is easy to get discouraged when things are going bad, but we shouldn't lose heart because God is at work in our lives even in the midst of pain and suffering.

Remember, next time your little hut is burning to the ground - it just may be a smoke signal that summons the intervention of God.

Since you have now seen all of these enemies of peace are self-inflicted, check out this little reflection on self-inflicted destruction of peace.

YOURSELF TO BLAME
by Mayme Miller

If things go bad for you and make you a bit ashamed,
Often you will find out that you have yourself to blame.
Swiftly we ran to mischief, and then this bad luck came.
Why do we fault others? We have ourselves to blame.
Whatever happens to us here is what we say:
"Had it not been for so-and-so things wouldn't have gone that way."
And if you are short of friends, I'll tell you what to do,
Make an examination, you'll find the fault is in you.
You are the captain of your ship, so agree with the same,
If you travel downward you have yourself to blame.

But, if you remember and truly believe "all things work for good", peace will come.

CHAPTER 9

THREE PEACE DESTROYING WORDS

I f you were to spend time in my counseling office, you would invariably hear me say, "There are three words I hate: **but**, **can't** and **feel**." Now I don't really hate those words, but I do hate them when they are negative and destructive to life and peace. If you really want to get me going, use them in the same sentence. "I know what God's Word says, BUT I FEEL that I CAN'T do what it says." Or, how about, "BUT I FEEL like God's Word doesn't apply to me, and I really CAN"T get past my feelings." As we proceed, I hope you will begin to understand the drastic effects these three words can have on our very own peace. In fact, you will begin to see how they become excuses for thoughts and behaviors destructive even to our very prospects for peace.

BUT

When used by us humans, the word "but" is mostly used in a negative context. This is a good thing, but! I would love that, but! It is used to put a negative spin, a negative edge on an otherwise positive statement. Come with me for an example taken from a marriage counseling session around Christmas time a few years ago.

The husband was very excited because he had purchased a surprise gift for his wife which he shared with me after the last session before the holidays. When they returned after Christmas I asked her if she had gotten anything special from her husband. I could see his face beam with pride. She replied he had surprised her by getting her something she had always wanted but had never asked for. I asked her what it was, and with a negative tone of voice she replied, "A reclining lounge chair complete with heat and massage." Again sensing the negative tone, I asked if it made her happy her husband had done that. "Yes, BUT it was the wrong color." So, I asked her what color it was, and she said "blue". Then I inquired as to what color she really wanted. I was shocked by her answer, "blue", and then she quickly added, "BUT, it was the wrong shade of blue."

Had you been sitting at my desk with me you would have readily observed the change in the husband's demeanor. He went from being swelled with pride to being completely deflated. With her "but", she had completely destroyed his peace, and without realizing it had affected her own as well.

See how destructive that little three-letter word can be. It can take a very pleasant, very peaceful situation and turn it into a moment of destruction. It becomes an excuse for my FEELING that things don't quite set right with me. Never mind others, it is completely self-focused. I have a short video clip entitled "Big Buts" which goes through a litany of reasons (buts) why we don't read our Bibles, serve at church, etc. All those BUTS are simply excuses so we can do our own thing, go our own way.

Fortunately for us, God uses "but" generally in a positive manner. *For the wages of sin is death,* **but** *the gift of God is eternal life in Christ Jesus our Lord* (Romans 6:23). I am eternally thankful for that "but", for without that, there would be no possibility for peace, only doom.

I CAN'T

Closely following a "but" is usually an "I can't". Do you realize how much damage you do to yourself every time you use that phrase? Every time it is uttered it becomes more deeply ingrained in your mind and belief system. Repeated often enough it becomes so firmly believed that whatever is being considered seems impossible.

If you are in my office and you use "I can't", I will counter with "won't" for that is the real truth. You will challenge me repeating you can't. I will then explain there are truly very few cant's in this life. I can perform brain surgery. It would be illegal, you would die, but I can do it. Certainly, there may be some things we can't do, but aren't we limiting God as well when we believe "I can't"?

After all, don't the Scriptures teach us that *With men this is impossible, but with God all things are possible* (Matthew 19:26), and *If you can believe, all things are possible to him who believes* (Mark 9:23). Those are the words of Jesus, not mine. The apostle Paul puts it this way *I can do all things through Christ who strengthens me* (Philippians 4:13). Seems like **if** it is God's will, then "I can't" is truly the "I won't" really meant by our statement which then becomes our excuse.

There are a few Biblical "cant's which we definitely need to be aware of:

Matthew 5:14 You are the light of the world. A city that is set on a hill cannot be hidden.

Matthew 7:18 A good tree cannot bear bad fruit, nor can a bad tree bear good fruit.

John 3:3 Jesus answered and said to him, "Most assuredly, I say to you, unless one is born again, he cannot see the kingdom of God."

So, we "can't" be saved without being born again, cannot hide our light, and cannot bear bad fruit when we are in God's hands and doing His will. But, if you will note, these "cant's" are also under God's control making them possible. Only our "I won't' can affect these principles.

"I can't" is the excuse we use to deflect responsibility for our own actions and choices. It helps foster the victim mentality which believes it is someone else's fault, and I need them or someone else to fix it for me or take responsibility for the situation. Even in Scripture we see the excuse of "I can't". When our Lord issued the parable of the great supper in Luke 14:15-24, He referred to three men who were bid to the feast. The first man had a "business" excuse; the second a "work" excuse. The third man had a "family" excuse, each of them saying simply, "I cannot (will not) come." Can you imagine telling the Lord Himself "I can't"? But in truth haven't you sometime in your life said, or at least thought, "I can't" when it comes to being obedient to and doing the will of your Savior?

The most damaging aspect of the "I can't" mentality is that it completely destroys hope. The rut is seen as too deep, the waters too muddy, the hill too steep to climb. Hope is shattered, and peace is gone, for it springs from and is sustained by hope. King Solomon in his wisdom put it thusly, *hope deferred makes the heart sick* (Proverbs 13:12). That sick heart then leads to a downward spiral which the prophet Jeremiah (18:12) described when he observed that *they said, "That is hopeless! So we will walk according to our own plans, and we will every one obey the dictates of his evil heart."* When Job (7:5-6) was in the midst of his suffering and focused on his circumstances he commented *My flesh is caked with worms and dust, My skin is cracked and breaks out afresh. My days are swifter than a weaver's shuttle, And are spent without hope.* No hope because the focus is on circumstances which bring out the "but, I can't". Focus clouded by those two phrases erases the prospect of "stayed upon Jehovah" which would bring peace.

When in one of his own "but, I can't" moods, David asked himself (Psalm 42:5), *Why are you cast down, O my soul? And why are you disquieted within me?* Then in the same verse he remembers the antidote: *Hope in God, for I shall yet praise Him for the help of His countenance.* Later David remembers the antidote of hope springs from the depths of God's Word. *Remember the word to Your servant, Upon which You have caused me to hope. This is my comfort in my affliction, For Your word has given me life* (Psalm 119:49-50).

I FEEL

Since Proverbs 23:7a says, *For as he thinks in his heart, so is he.* The indication is that our feelings flow from our thinking. Therefore, it should be fairly easy to surmise faulty "but, I can't" thinking leads to those feelings of anger, guilt, anxiety, despair, etc. that literally take control of us. The feelings appear so real because they result from our destructive thought patterns. I think angry thoughts so I feel angry, and I know what the Word of God says about anger, but I can't do anything about it because I feel angry. What a vicious cycle!

Paul says (Romans 8:8) *So then, those who are in the flesh cannot please God.* "In the flesh" - controlled by feelings, or as we saw in Jeremiah "we walk according to our own plans" and "obey the dictates" of our evil hearts. Where does that come from? "But, I can't because I feel." So, we think, we feel, we focus on our feelings, we think some more, our feelings worsen and "I can't" becomes a reality to our minds. Yet in truth it is nothing but a figment of our imagination.

We become impatient, focusing on our circumstance and lose our perspective, and even begin to doubt the truth of God's Word. We even especially get upset with ideas like "all things work together for good" (Romans 8:28), and that God will not "tempt us above what we are able" (I Corinthians 10:13). We certainly "can't" "give thanks in everything" (I Thessalonians 5:18) , "count it all joy" (James 1:2), or "rejoice evermore" (I Thessalonians 5:16) because we don't "feel" like it.

Yet according to Paul we can be *rejoicing in hope, patient in tribulation, continuing steadfastly in prayer* (Romans 12:12) because *this hope we have as an anchor of the soul, both sure and steadfast* (Hebrews 6:19). So, my friend, *be of good courage, and He shall strengthen your heart, all you who hope in the Lord* (Psalm 31:24).

If you are burdened with "but I can't feelings" I leave you with this benediction. *Now may our Lord Jesus Christ Himself, and our God and Father, who has loved us and given us everlasting consolation and good hope by grace, comfort your hearts and establish you in every good word and work* (II Thessalonians 2:16-17).

There is one other way "I feel" or Paul's "in the flesh" disturbs our peace. However, it does not flow from the mode of "I can't", rather from a standpoint of "I can." It is the search for peace in people, places, and things we "feel" will bring us pleasure or peace. Even for Christians there can be a diversion from obedience to God in this pursuit of peace that is fueled by our "wanter". In fact, today's mantra can be summed up in a couple of popular sayings. "If it feels good, do it." The other simply says, "follow your heart." Didn't Paul even say that all things were legal in I Corinthians?

Thus, the philosophy goes: I can get drunk, I can have sex outside of marriage, I can get high on drugs, I can be a homosexual or transgender, etc., etc. All driven by my search for inner peace and satisfaction coming from a heart that according to Jeremiah 17:9 is "deceitful and desperately wicked." BUT, I FEEL like these things will bring peace to my troubled soul, and since I CAN, I will try them out.

However, these attractions are temporary and transitory in their ability to bring even a sense of false peace, for they are subject to the law of diminishing returns. In other words, they have to be repeated over and over, done faster, harder, kinkier, longer, to get the same effect. Even then the "feeling" is gone in a moment, and gone with it is the false sense of peace to only be replaced by a sense of guilt, anger, anxiety, etc. Now I need more peace, so I need to do it again, and again, and again. To me, that sounds like a prescription for addiction. Could that be why Paul, after saying "all things are lawful for me", went on to say, "but I will not be brought under the power of any" (I Corinthians 6:12)? Seems as if he recognized the danger of following our feelings in the search for peace.

That feeling of "power" can also not only lead to addiction but can also lead to a momentary lapse of judgment which can destroy our peace. Let me illustrate with an incident that took place several years ago. I was traveling and singing with an evangelist for a set of meetings, when one night he arrived at the church in a rather agitated state. I asked him what was the problem. He replied he had just stopped at the red light at the bottom of the hill. The car ahead of him had a bumper sticker that read "If it feels good, do it." He said what he felt like doing at that moment was to put his car in reverse, back up, put his car in drive, floor the gas pedal, ram into the back of that car and yell "that sure felt good."

In analyzing the situation, he was feeling angry, yet guilty for feeling that way. Ashamed he had those thoughts and feelings - definitely not at peace. Yet, he was free to do as he felt had he been "brought under the power" of those feelings. How many times do we succumb to a feeling that we allow to overpower us? Believe it or not, I have had people in my counseling office tell me things like "I know my adultery is okay by God, because I have prayed and feel complete peace about it." The "wanter", the feeling so powerful it overcomes obedience to the Word and will of God in our lives. There will never be peace under those conditions.

In his other comment about things being lawful (I Corinthians 10:23), Paul said that, though lawful, they might not be helpful or edifying. They will not be helpful in bringing us peace. If they are not edifying us or others, they will not bring us peace. So don't let "but, can't, and feelings" get in your way on the path to peace.

CHAPTER 10

THE PEACE OF ASSURANCE

The issue of assurance, or as it is often called, the eternal security of the believer, could have probably been included in one of the previous chapters of "The Enemies of Peace", but is such an important matter it deserved its own special attention. So, allow me to put it into a specific statement: You cannot have the "peace of God" if you do not believe in the eternal security of the believer. I realize this is a strong statement with which many will disagree, but to me it follows as a natural result from the establishment of peace at its very beginning.

If you agree with my earlier premise stating one must first have "peace **WITH** God" in order to find the "peace **OF** God", then does it not follow that anything which would disrupt "peace with God" would disrupt the "peace of God"? What could be more disrupting or unsettling to the mind and soul than to not be sure at any given moment whether or not you have "peace with God"? If you agree we cannot earn our salvation, if you agree we do not deserve our salvation, because it is the gift of God (Ephesians 2:8-9), what makes you think you can "keep" your salvation by some "works" since we can still commit sin. I believe our eternal security, like our salvation, is a gift from God.

This will not be a long theological debate attempting to persuade you as to the "correctness" of my own personal views, but rather to share with you some practical considerations from the Word of God which I hold dear. Therefore, I would simply ask you to very prayerfully and thoughtfully consider each of the verses of scripture which follow.

> These things I have written to you who believe in the
> name of the Son of God, that you **may know** that you
> have **eternal life**, and that you may continue to believe
> in the name of the Son of God. (I John 5:13, emphasis mine)

There are two definite things to consider from this verse which are pertinent to the idea of eternal security. First, John says these things were written that we might KNOW. Second, he goes on to tell us what we can know, which is "that you HAVE eternal life". Big deal you say, so what. Well, it is an eternal deal. Ponder this question:

WHAT IS ETERNAL LIFE? Your answer is probably something like: "Everlasting, it goes on forever." Right!! But if you can lose it, is it eternal?

> Most assuredly, I say to you, he who hears My word and
> believes in Him who sent Me **has** everlasting life, and
> **shall not come into judgment**, but has passed from death
> into life. (John 5:24, emphasis mine)

Here again, we are faced with the concept of "everlasting life", plus this verse adds two more thought-provoking ideas. When do we get this eternal life? This verse indicates we receive it at the moment of our salvation, not later in a progression of events. We have it right now! Also this verse states very plainly we "shall not come into judgment". Would not God have to perform some sort of judgment to determine if we should lose our salvation because of a certain sin, a certain group of sins, or length of time spent in sin? This idea is also presented as:

> There is therefore now no condemnation to those who
> are in Christ Jesus... (Romans 8:1a)

So, who is not judged? The saved (those in Christ Jesus). What happens to them?

No condemnation!

Look also at the beautiful picture of the relationship between the sheep and their Shepherd painted by the Apostle John.

> My sheep hear My voice, and I know them, and they
> follow Me. And I give them **eternal life**, and they shall
> **never perish; neither shall anyone snatch them out
> of My hand.** My Father, who has given them to Me,
> is greater than all; and **no one is able to snatch them
> out of My Father's hand.** (John 10:27-29, emphasis mine)

What a place of security! Not only eternal life, not only a place where we shall not perish, but safe in the hands of our Lord and Savior. The picture is of us resting in His grasp, or in the palm of His hand, from which NO MAN can snatch us out. Wow! And, as if that were not safe enough, the Father's hand is securely wrapped around the hand of His Son, with a double guarantee from the God, who cannot lie, that NO MAN is able to snatch us out. Double Wow! Think about what this really means. Are you a man (or woman)? If so, then how can you (or anyone else) snatch yourself from the hand of Almighty God when He say you cannot?

Having now considered the working of the Father and His only Son in our redemptive security, what about the Holy Spirit? Does He play a part in this security as well? Just listen:

> In Him you also trusted, after you heard the word of truth,
> the gospel of your salvation; in whom also, having believed,
> you were **sealed with the Holy Spirit of promise**, who is the
> **guarantee of our inheritance** until the redemption of the
> **purchased possession**, to the praise of His glory.
> (Ephesians 1:13-14, emphasis mine)

I believe there are three important considerations here. First, we are **sealed** when we believe (the moment of salvation), not at some later date "when we deserve or have earned it" because of works or faithfulness. Second, we are **sealed** by the Holy Spirit - a seal that separates us, sets us apart for God, and distinguishes and marks us as belonging to Him. And third, the Holy Spirit is the **guarantee** of our inheritance. The payment has been made and is guaranteed. Is God's guarantee revocable?

I said there were three points, but yet another appears, which is the idea of the **purchased possession**. The word "possession" by its very nature points once again to the fact we already belong to God. We are His, and His FOREVER.

Then there is the idea of adoption. In the Greek and Roman cultures prevalent at the time of the writing of the New Testament, the laws of adoption were quite emphatic on this issue. You could disinherit a natural born son, but you **could not disinherit** an adopted son. Could this be why God uses this term to apply to the state of our salvation. Just look at some of the Scriptures regarding this issue of adoption.

Roman 8:15 We have not received a spirit of fear, but of adoption as sons.

Romans 8:16 Spirit bears witness that we are children of God.

Romans 8:17 We are heirs, and joint-heirs with Christ.

Ephesians 1:5 We are predestined unto adoption.

Galatians 4:5 We receive adoption as sons.

Then there is the issue of marriage, since God likens our relationship to His Son as just like a bride to her husband.

> For I am jealous for you with godly jealousy. For I have
> betrothed you to one husband, that I may present you as
> a chaste virgin to Christ. (II Corinthians 11:2)

With this picture, think about God's view of divorce. He sees the marriage as a covenant relationship which endures, lasts despite performance, etc. In essence, God HATES divorce (Malachi 2:16). Thus, would God ever divorce us, or disinherit one of His children?

Having promised this would not be a long theological debate, let me close with a look at my personal favorite passage of Scripture which really says it all for me.

> Blessed be the God and Father of our Lord Jesus Christ,
> who according to His abundant mercy has begotten us
> again to a living hope through the resurrection of Jesus
> Christ from the dead, to an inheritance incorruptible and
> undefiled and that does not fade away, reserved in heaven
> for you, who are kept by the power of God through faith for salvation
> ready to be revealed in the last time. In this you
> greatly rejoice… (I Peter 1:3-6a)

There are several precious thoughts to be garnered from this great passage regarding the eternal security of the believer;

- It is God's mercy which saves and keeps us.
- We have an inheritance (eternal life).
- This inheritance is incorruptible. It cannot rot or decay (Unger).
- Our inheritance is undefiled, "I.e. from that by which the nature of a thing is deformed, pure from sin" (Unger). Our propensity to sin, even sin itself cannot mar it.
- Neither time nor action can make it fade.
- It is reserved in heaven for you. Your name is already on the door of a mansion. This is confirmed by Paul who states "our citizenship is in heaven" (Philippians 3:20).

- And most importantly, we are kept just as we are saved, not by our works or efforts, but by the power of God.

Praise the Lord! In this you can greatly rejoice. You have "peace with God" forever and can bask in the blessing of "the peace of God" as you walk through this life.

CHAPTER 11

THE FALSE PEACE

As the result of things I had heard during a couple of counseling sessions, I felt constrained to write another chapter as it pertains to many people who "feel" they have peace in their situation. However, I fear it is not real peace coming from God, but rather a false peace coming from justification of sinful choices. Maybe the best way to approach this subject is to allow you to analyze along with me the following scenario, or similar ones, which have sadly played more times than I can count in my office.

The client (a professing Christian) has left her husband and is involved in an adulterous affair. Listen as she responds to my Biblical exhortation and rebuke.

> "But I have complete peace about leaving my husband.
> It has been so peaceful with the new man. Besides, my new
> situation (adultery) is so good that it can't possibly be
> wrong. I have prayed, and God has given me complete
> peace about it. After all, God must be in it, we met
> at church."

Before analyzing this statement, I must let you know at this point I roll my chair back as far away as I can from people like this, while I explain to them that what they have just said is blasphemy, and I want to be just as far away from them as I can just in case the Lord sends a lightning bolt through the window.

Now, in analyzing her statement I can find at least four indications or types of "false peace".

1. Absence of conflict.
2. I want.
3. Justifiable circumstances.
4. Answered prayer.

Many people express a feeling of peace, but when their situation is explored, they are only talking about an absence of an immediate sense of conflict. Surely there is a sense of peace, when nothing is going wrong at the moment, because God's peace will last, will prevail in the midst of any storm. It is easy sometimes to ignore the voice of the Holy Spirit and thus feel like there is peace. So be careful to determine, since you are not in the middle of turmoil, whether you have real peace from God, not just an absence of conflict in the moment.

Others simply WANT something so badly they will have it no matter what God's Word says. The "want" is so strong that once achieved, the mind can go to great lengths to not heed or rationalize away Holy Spirit conviction. This way the sinful situation appears to be legitimized and "right" because it feels so good or some other foolish rationalization. The strength of the "want" (now perceived as a need) is the basis for the "peace" which is felt. This is a lie from the pit of hell, not peace from God.

I believe King Solomon had the great emotional power of a "want" in mind when he penned:

> The backslider in heart will be filled with his own ways...
> (Proverbs 14:14a)

Two verses earlier he also cautioned us regarding the direction and result of such a "want' outside of God's will:

There is a way that seems right to a man, But its end is
the way of death. (Proverbs 14:12)

Does this sound like the way to find peace? False peace, based on something "I want" and then get, can leave me with far more than I bargained for, less than I deserve, and certainly not God's peace.

Then comes the circumstantial - the circumstances were right so God must be in it (we met at church). After all, if God hadn't wanted it this way, why did He have it happen, or why didn't He stop it? Time to roll the chair back again! Are you involving God in your adultery? She was quite shocked to find Satan is very capable of arranging such a meeting as well. So, if you think this "peace" came from God you need to consider:

Let no one say when he is tempted, "I am tempted by God";
for God cannot be tempted by evil, nor does He Himself
tempt anyone. James 1:13

In fact, the very next verse says very emphatically: "But each one is tempted when he is **drawn away by his own desires** and enticed (James 1:14, emphasis mine), which brings us right back to the previous false sense of peace brought about by "I want".

We saw back in chapter 8 how prayer could be an "enemy of peace", and a supplier of false peace as well. You may ask, "How can prayer be the precursor to false peace?" Possibly the manner in which we pray, or even the seeming answer to our prayer may be instrumental in bringing us a false sense of peace. Allow me to explain.

First, consider linking prayer with "I want" and then receiving the fulfillment of such a request. God has seemingly answered your prayer, so why should you not be at peace. If you are like the client who had peace with her adultery, you should know why. But just to make sure, remember "praying to consume it upon your lusts" is never going to bring peace from God. If you perhaps prayed aloud about this, who else was listening and would love to answer an "I want" sinful prayer? That's right - Satan, and he delights in giving us our requests, especially when they are sinful. He is a deceiver and a destroyer, who would like nothing better than to have us at "peace" in a sinful situation.

Also, if you are in the habit of praying and using some sort of fleece (circumstantial) to determine God's will, or your peace, Satan is again very delighted to oblige. These forms of "peace" may very well come from Satan, the master counterfeiter, not from our loving God.

There may be an occasion when God does answer an "I want" prayer which is not sinful in nature because He is a loving God. However, He may also answer one of these prayers which is not His will because we persist in praying despite indications God has already answered (no), and we don't like or accept His answer, so we keep praying and praying. He may use the answer as a teaching tool to show us He knows best and our "want" may not be right for us or what we really need. Remember the children of Israel who "lusted exceedingly in the wilderness" (Psalm 106:14)? What happened?

> And He gave them their request, But sent leanness into
> their soul. (Psalm 106:15)

They got what they "wanted" but found it hollow, unfulfilling, with no peace to be had.

The old saying goes: "A rose is rose, is a rose, is a rose", but peace is not peace just because we seem to feel it. We need to be discerning for "Beloved, do not believe every spirit, but test the spirits, whether they are of God" (I John 4:1a), and beware:

> For when they say, "Peace and safety!" then sudden
> destruction comes upon them, as labor pains upon a
> pregnant woman. And they shall not escape.
> (I Thessalonians 5:3)

We need only to remember as my dear Father used to say: "sin will take you farther than you want to go; cost you more than you can afford; and keep you longer than you want to stay." That does not sound like a peaceful prospect because "sin destroys peace".

Be at peace, but make sure it comes from God.

CHAPTER 12

THE ART OF PEACEMAKING

All of us want to have peace in our lives, and so we may go to great lengths to keep the peace whenever the situation becomes less than peaceful. However, does the Word of God tell us to keep the peace or to make peace? Is there a difference between peacekeeping and peacemaking?

To see if there is a difference, let's start with the famous Mr. Webster who seems to know what words mean.

Peacekeeper - one that keeps or protects the peace.

Peacemaker - one who makes peace especially by reconciling parties at variance.

Both sound pretty good, and both are better than the alternative, but they are different and one is actually blessed by God.

So let's start with the "peacekeeper", the one who is always trying to make things better. But how does he do it? Well, the "keeper" tries to achieve the peace by maintaining it with two basic methods. His first method is "avoidance", which means he/she will go to great lengths to avoid unpleasant, unmerciful situations. He will go to great lengths to avoid people, places or situations which might have the potential for less than peaceful outcomes. For example, getting invited to a family gathering knowing there is a cousin coming with whom there has been past conflict. Peace is attempted by not going at all or doing their best to avoid any contact with that cousin. To put it in not so pleasant terms, it is foolish to believe peace will be kept if they avoid the situation, and there is an absence of any conflict .

The second aspect of "peacekeeping" is what I would call appeasement. This means they will smooth over the ruffled feathers, give in, or pretend it doesn't matter. This is a "peace at any cost" attitude which sounds pretty good, but for most of us cannot be sustained forever. There comes a point where we feel like we can't take any more, and the lid comes off. We have reached the boiling point and explode. Passivity and giving in seem to work, but not forever.

The main problem with "peacekeeping' is it is entirely one-sided. I bend over backwards, and you keep pushing - not a prescription for lasting peace. The peacekeeper believes by ignoring, simply overlooking, or by smoothing over problems, peace has been accomplished.

That brings us to "peacemaking" and some ideas of why do it, how to do it, and why it is more effective and more long-lasting.

First of all, "peacemaking" is blessed by God for *Blessed are the peacemakers, For they shall be called sons of God* (Matthew 5:9). Blessed, meaning happy, because of the lack of conflict, or at least the ability to weather the storm, and blessed because of obedience to God. The peacemaker, instead of keeping the peace, attempts to actually make peace which will last. He/she does it in the three following manners.

First, the peacemaker is completely honest about the issues. He is not afraid to let you know what you did or said, didn't do or say which upset him, but couples it with an offer to make it right. This may sound unkind or selfish, but he knows, unlike the peacekeeper, if the issue is not dealt with there will come a peace-disturbing incident ahead. Therefore, he will confront the issue head on in order to maintain or re-establish peace very quickly. He firmly believes God's admonition to "Recompense to no man evil for evil. Provide things honest in the sight of all men" (Romans 12:17, KJV). In fact, like the writer of Hebrews, he would ask you to pray for him so he would "have a good conscience, in all things willing to live honestly" (Hebrews 13:18, KJV).

This is probably because he realizes unity is not the same as harmony; they are not exactly the same. Are you confused? Let me share a simple example: my wife and I are a unity; we are married and in God's eyes we are one. However, the moment we disagree on something, harmony is gone. Mr. Webster makes a distinction as well for he says unity is the "state of being one". He goes on to define harmony as "accord (agreement) in feeling, sentiment, etc." So, you can see you can have one without the other. Putting this into a church context as well, you may be a member (unity), but the moment you disagree with something the pastor says or some new program, the harmony is disrupted.

The peacemaker firmly believes the scriptural principle "If it is possible, as much as **depends on you**, live peaceably with all men" (Romans 12:18, emphasis mine). Therefore, he is not afraid to confront issues before they get out of hand. He would choose to face an issue rather than "sweep it under the rug" as the peacekeeper would do.

Second, the peacemaker will be quick to apologize for his part in the incident. He knows the best way to re-establish peace is to admit any wrongdoing or misconception on his behalf. His spiritual guideline for this sort of thinking would come from "And be kind to one another, tenderhearted, forgiving one another, even as God in Christ forgave you" (Ephesians 4:32). He fully believes in the power of forgiveness: to forgive you if you have wronged him, confessing, and seeking forgiveness if he has wronged you.

He will combine the first step of honesty with the second step of forgiveness as instructed by the apostle Paul. "Bearing with one another, and forgiving one another, if anyone has a complaint against another; even as Christ forgave you, so you also must do"(Colossians 3:13). He will "bear with" until he realizes there is a problem since he has "a complaint against another", but he will either seek or give forgiveness depending on his side of the issue. His basis for such action - "as Christ forgave you, so you must also do".

When he combines these steps, the peacemaker has embarked upon the third necessary step to re-establish peace - he will pursue reconciliation. In other words, he wants to re-establish peace (unity and harmony) rather than simply let it pass. Again, he is following the Biblical mandate of reconciliation.

Therefore, if anyone is in Christ, he is a new creation; old things
have passed away; behold, all things have become new.
Now all things are of God, who has reconciled us to Himself through
Jesus Christ, and **has given us the ministry of reconciliation**,
that is, that God was in Christ reconciling the world to Himself, not
imputing their trespasses to them, and has **committed to us the
word of reconciliation**.
Now then, we are ambassadors for Christ, as though God were
pleading through us: we implore you on Christ's behalf, be reconciled
to God. (II Corinthians 5:17-20, emphasis mine)

I realize much of the ministry of reconciliation deals with our
reaching the lost with the Gospel of Christ to reconcile them to God.
However, if it were restricted to just that, would we be good ambassadors
if the lost see that we, as Christians, can't get along, that we have lost
our harmony, thus affecting our unity?

In short, I believe the differences between the keeper and the maker
could be summed up thusly. I am not saying all peacekeeping is bad, but
the problem remains, can peace be kept forever, given our fallen natures.
The peacekeeper simply believes peace is the absence of problems and
thus avoids them. The peacemaker would agree in essence with this
belief but would know peace is not just the absence of problems, but
real peace is the presence of Jesus. Therefore, he would rather make
peace which can have eternal results than merely keep a peace which
may not last.

Therefore let us **pursue the things which make for peace**
and the things by which one may edify another.
(Romans 14:19, emphasis mine)

Now the fruit of righteousness is sown in peace by those
who make peace. (James 3:18, emphasis mine)

CHAPTER 13

THE DISRUPTION OF PEACE

As I was putting, I thought, the finishing touches on this book, we were struck by the Corona virus pandemic. The world has been drastically affected by shut downs of economies, people confined to their homes and thousands dying. Certainly trying times! It is during times like this when many begin to wonder about the "goodness of God". How could a loving God let things like this happen? Peace has been disrupted; why hasn't God stepped in and fixed it? Most of what I have discussed about peace so far had to do with how we, by our own sinful choices, disrupt our peace. But what about those circumstances beyond our control, those not caused by our sin? So, let's again look to the Word of God and see why and if, God has anything to say about situations caused by or at least allowed by Him.

With so much extra time on our hands, my wife and I watched the movie "The Hiding Place", the story of holocaust survivor Corrie Ten Boom. She was a Christian girl who felt God would have her and her family aid their Jewish neighbors and friends by helping them hide from and escape Nazi tyranny. Of course, they were eventually found out and sent to the very concentration camp intended for those Jews. Most of her family died; she survived but suffered terrible indignities and harm, so much so that her faith at times seemed to waiver. Some of the Jewish ladies with which they were imprisoned challenged her and her sister with questions like those I posed in the opening paragraph. But through it all, her faith was strengthened; her testimony eventually led some to the Lord, and later, she was released. Corrie then spent the rest of her life traveling the world testifying to God's grace and love. Did she learn something about undeserved disruptions of peace? Did she understand how her God could "work all things for good"? Let me share with you her summation of her experiences: "No pit is so deep, that He is not deeper".

In more modern times, there is Joni Eareckson Tada. If you are not familiar with her story, she was paralyzed from the neck down as a teenager in a diving accident while swimming with friends. Then after years as a quadriplegic, she has now endured two bouts with cancer. How could she still smile? How could life go on? How could she ever continue to love and serve the God who allowed these tragedies in her life? Allow me to share from one of her pamphlets (*Making Sense of Suffering*) her observation:

> "Even as we approach the subject of suffering with the aid of God's Word, we find the complete "why" behind pain and problems is never found. Instead, we discover we must rest on the character of God, trusting that all suffering takes place within His sovereignty."

Then from another pamphlet (*Facing Trials With Joy*) observe her prospective on how God's disruption of her peace has played out in her life.

> Many verses "in the Bible seem to guarantee that God should protect us from harmful, hurtful things, So why would God allow a quadriplegic chronic pain, and then two vicious rounds with cancer? The answer: God is less interested in my physical well-being and more interested in strengthening my soul...But the kindness of His sovereignty is the good that's being accomplished in my soul: a stronger faith, a deeper wisdom, an **increase of peace** (emphasis mine), a higher joy,

an unwavering devotion to Christ, and the ironclad trust that comes from walking through that valley of the shadow of death."

Well and good you say, but what about the Bible? Did anyone of God's people suffer because of God's sovereign action in their lives and not as a result of their sinful choices? Did those situations turn "out for good?" Let's take a quick look at four men who suffered unjustly, allowed by God, but not because of their sinful thoughts or actions - Joseph, Job, Paul, and our Lord Himself.

Way back in the book of Genesis we find a young man named Joseph whose problem was that he shared a God-given dream with his brothers who were already jealous of their father's seeming preference for the young lad. So, one day they threw him in a well and then sold him into slavery to a roving band of men headed for Egypt. How could that be good? How could God allow it? Well, he gets to Egypt and is purchased by a man named Potiphar and goes to work. One day Potiphar's wife makes sexual advances towards him which he refuses. In her response to his rejection of her offer she lies to her husband saying Joseph had tried to rape her. Off to jail, falsely accused.

Again, where was his loving God when his actions were not sinful, in fact he was obeying God with the choice he made. Sometime later his brothers come to Egypt and meet up with Joseph, and they are afraid for he is now a powerful man. He can kill us, or he can put us in jail, were the kinds of thoughts running through their heads. But Joseph responds: "you meant evil against me; but **God meant it for good**, in order to bring it about as it is this day, to save many people alive." (Genesis 50:20, emphasis mine)

Next, we see Job who "was perfect and upright, and one that feared God, and shunned evil" (Job 1:1). Then along comes Satan and challenges God saying Job only served him because nothing bad had ever happened to him. Well, if you know the story, you know he then lost his herds, his house, his children and suffered physically as well. His wife, who should have been supporting him, even comes against him when she says, "Curse God, and die" (Job 2:9). Then he gets wrongfully accused by friends who also should have been a source of support. How does Job react to all this undeserved calamity? Listen to his summation: "He knows the way that I take; when he has tested me, I shall come forth as gold…for he performs the thing that is appointed for me" (Job 2:10, 14).

Moving to the New Testament, we find Paul. Just look at a few of the underserved trials which he endured in II Corinthians 11:23-28.

> Are they ministers of Christ?–I speak as a fool–I am more: in labors more abundant, in stripes above measure, in prisons more frequently, in deaths often.
> From the Jews five times I received forty stripes minus one.
> Three times I was beaten with rods; once I was stoned; three times I was shipwrecked; a night and a day I have been in the deep;
> in journeys often, in perils of waters, in perils of robbers, in perils of my own countrymen, in perils of the Gentiles, in perils in the city, in perils in the wilderness, in perils in the sea, in perils among false brethren;
> in weariness and toil, in sleeplessness often, in hunger and thirst, in fastings often, in cold and nakedness.

What was his reaction to his undeserved trials? Well it was Romans 8:28 stating that "all things work for good", and Philippians 4:11b where he states "I have learned, in whatever state I am, in this to be content". Sounds like undeserved trials strengthened rather than undermined his faith.

Check out the story of the blind man.

> Now as Jesus passed by, He saw a man who was blind from birth. And His disciples asked Him, saying, "Rabbi, who sinned, this man or his parents, that he was born blind?"

Jesus answered, "Neither this man nor his parents sinned, but **that the works of God should be revealed in him**." (John 9:1-3, emphasis mine)

Lastly, what about our dear Savior? He suffered terrible indignities, pain, and even death for us. Did he deserve it? Was it his fault? Had he done anything wrong? NO, a thousand times NO!

For Christ also suffered once for sins, the just for the unjust, that He might bring us to God, being put to death in the flesh but made alive by the Spirit. (1 Peter 3:18)

For we do not have a High Priest who cannot sympathize with our weaknesses, but was in all points tempted as we are, yet without sin. Let us therefore come boldly to the throne of grace, that we may obtain mercy and find grace to help in time of need. (Hebrews 4:15-16)

He suffered, bled and died for you!

Yet here we are, grumble and complain when things don't go our way, things aren't just right. We are probably more apt to take suffering when we know our sin caused it.

For what credit is it if, when you are beaten for your faults, you take it patiently? But when you do good and suffer, if you take it patiently, this is commendable before God. For to this you were called, because Christ also suffered for us, leaving us an example, that you should follow His steps: "Who committed no sin, Nor was deceit found in His mouth"; who, when He was reviled, did not revile in return; when He suffered, He did not threaten, but committed Himself to Him who judges righteously. (1 Peter 2:20-23)

So why would storms ever come? What do we do when a tornado blows down our house, a drunk driver totals our new car, or we find out we have cancer? Can we even begin to understand why God would allow such things? We don't like it, but we understand when God has to chastise us for our sinful choices which have gone without confession and repentance. But why, oh why do bad things happen to good people? When I reflect on such things, I think of my Uncle Mark and Aunt Gladys who spent their lives on the mission field serving the Lord. Then in 1969 on their way to minister in a church in Iran where they were serving, a car accident took the lives of their three children. My uncle's reaction when I talked with him on the phone: "Your aunt Gladys and I could not be any closer to the Lord at this moment, even if we had the children back." That blew me away but helped in my acceptance of and learning about the reasons God allows or brings trials into our lives. In fact, ponder the significance of the following verses.

> Beloved, **do not think it strange** concerning the fiery trial which is to try you, as though some strange thing happened to you; but **rejoice** to the extent that you partake of Christ's sufferings, that when His glory is revealed, you may also be **glad with exceeding joy**. If you are reproached for the name of Christ, **blessed are you**, for the Spirit of glory and of God rests upon you. On their part He is blasphemed, but on your part He is glorified. ... Yet if anyone suffers as a Christian, let him not be ashamed, but let him glorify God in this matter. (1 Peter 4:12-14, 16, emphasis mine)

> For it is better, if it is the will of God, to suffer for doing good than for doing evil. (1 Peter 3:17)

Rejoice, be glad, blessed, better to suffer for doing good? How can this be? Especially when we don't understand the mind and ways of our God, it is so hard to understand. So, does God's Word shed any light on the how and why we might suffer when it is not because of our sin? I want you to think of it this way as we search the Scriptures. Storms come into our lives, and sometimes they are a bit inconvenient - we get a little wet getting to the car or into the house. Sometimes they ruin a picnic with friends or family. Sometimes they are catastrophic and flood our home or blow off our roof. Keeping storms (over which we have no control and are not due to our choices) in mind let's see if we can figure out why God allows or even causes storms in our lives. I will not add much commentary but will allow His Word to speak for Him.

God allows/brings storms into our lives to get our attention and increase our witness.

You, who have shown me great and severe troubles, Shall revive me again, And bring me up again from the depths of the earth. You shall increase my greatness, And comfort me on every side. ... My tongue also shall talk of Your righteousness all the day long; For they are confounded, For they are brought to shame Who seek my hurt. (Psalm 71:20-21, 24)

God allows/brings storms into our lives to exhibit His power and sovereignty.

For He has delivered me out of all trouble; And my eye has seen its desire upon my enemies. (Psalm 54:7)

God allows/brings storms into our lives to reveal Himself to us.

Therefore behold, I will this once cause them to know, I will cause them to know My hand and My might; And they shall know that My name is the LORD. (Jeremiah 16:21)

I am the LORD, and there is no other; There is no God besides Me. I will gird you, though you have not known Me, That they may know from the rising of the sun to its setting That there is none besides Me. I am the LORD, and there is no other; I form the light and **create darkness**, I make peace and **create calamity**; I, the LORD, do all these things. (Isaiah 45:5-7, emphasis mine)

God allows/brings storms into our lives to remind us He is in control.

For My thoughts are not your thoughts, Nor are your ways My ways, says the LORD. For as the heavens are higher than the earth, So are My ways higher than your ways, And My thoughts than your thoughts. For as the rain comes down, and the snow from heaven, And do not return there, But water the earth, And make it bring forth and bud, That it may give seed to the sower And bread to the eater, So shall My word be that goes forth from My mouth; It shall not return to Me void, But it shall accomplish what I please, And it shall prosper in the thing for which I sent it. (Isaiah 55:8-11)

O house of Israel, can I not do with you as this potter? says the LORD. "Look, as the clay is in the potter's hand, so are you in My hand, O house of Israel! (Jeremiah 18:6)

God allows/brings storms into our lives to show how help from man is vain.

Thus says the LORD: Cursed is the man who trusts in man and makes flesh his strength, Whose heart departs from the LORD. (Jeremiah 17:5)

God allows/brings storms into our lives to bring us His power.

And He said to me, "My grace is sufficient for you, for My
strength is made perfect in weakness." Therefore most gladly
I will rather boast in my infirmities, that the power of Christ
may rest upon me. Therefore I take pleasure in infirmities,
in reproaches, in needs, in persecutions, in distresses, for Christ's
sake. For when I am weak, then I am strong. (2 Corinthians 12:9-10)

God allows/brings storms into our lives to bring Him glory.

For behold, the darkness shall cover the earth, And deep darkness
the people; But the LORD will arise over you, And His glory will
be seen upon you. (Isaiah 60:2)

In this you greatly rejoice, though now for a little while, if need be,
you have been grieved by various trials, that the genuineness of
your faith, being much more precious than gold that perishes, though
it is tested by fire, may be found to praise, honor, and glory at the
revelation of Jesus Christ. (1 Peter 1:6-7)

Yet if anyone suffers as a Christian, let him not be ashamed,
but let him glorify God in this matter. (1 Peter 4:16)

For I consider that the sufferings of this present time are not
worthy to be compared with the glory which shall be revealed
in us.
(Romans 8:18)

God allows/brings storms into our lives to increase our faith.

He will not be afraid of evil tidings; His heart is steadfast,
trusting in the LORD. His heart is established; He will not
be afraid, Until he sees his desire upon his enemies.
(Psalm 112:7-8)

If you faint in the day of adversity, Your strength is small.
(Proverbs 24:10)

God is our refuge and strength, A very present help in trouble.
Therefore we will not fear, Even though the earth be removed,
And though the mountains be carried into the midst of the sea.
(Psalm 46:1-2)

God allows/brings storms into our lives to teach us patience.

And not only that, but we also glory in tribulations, knowing
that tribulation produces perseverance; and perseverance,
character; and character, hope. (Romans 5:3-4)

My brethren, count it all joy when you fall into various trials,
knowing that the testing of your faith produces patience.
But let patience have its perfect work, that you may be perfect
and complete, lacking nothing. (James 1:2-4)

God allows/brings storms into our lives to refine us.

For You, O God, have tested us; You have refined us as silver
is refined. You brought us into the net; You laid affliction on
our backs. You have caused men to ride over our heads; We
went through fire and through water; But You brought us out
to rich fulfillment. (Psalm 66:10-12)

Behold, I have refined you, but not as silver; I have tested you
in the furnace of affliction. (Isaiah 48:10)

God allows/brings storms into our lives to test the quality of our works.

> According to the grace of God which was given to me, as a wise master builder I have laid the foundation, and another builds on it. But let each one take heed how he builds on it. For no other foundation can anyone lay than that which is laid, which is Jesus Christ. Now if anyone builds on this foundation with gold, silver, precious stones, wood, hay, straw, each one's work will become clear; for the Day will declare it, because it will be revealed by fire; and the fire will test each one's work, of what sort it is. (1 Corinthians 3:10-13)

God allows/brings storms into our lives to chasten us.

> But when we are judged, we are chastened by the Lord, that we may not be condemned with the world. (1 Corinthians 11:32)

> And you have forgotten the exhortation which speaks to you as to sons: My son, do not despise the chastening of the LORD, Nor be discouraged when you are rebuked by Him. (Hebrews 12:5)

> Now no chastening seems to be joyful for the present, but painful; nevertheless, afterward it yields the peaceable fruit of righteousness to those who have been trained by it. (Hebrews 12:11)

God allows/brings storms into our lives to bring us to repentance.

> Now I rejoice, not that you were made sorry, but that your sorrow led to repentance. For you were made sorry in a godly manner, that you might suffer loss from us in nothing. For godly sorrow produces repentance leading to salvation, not to be regretted; but the sorrow of the world produces death. (2 Corinthians 7:9-10)

133

As many as I love, I rebuke and chasten. Therefore be zealous and repent. (Revelation 3:19)

God allows/brings storms into our lives to conform us to His image.

For whom He foreknew, He also predestined to be conformed to the image of His Son, that He might be the firstborn among many brethren. (Romans 8:29)

God allows/brings storms into our lives so we bear fruit.

Every branch in Me that does not bear fruit He takes away; and every branch that bears fruit He prunes, that it may bear more fruit. (John 15:2)

God allows/brings storms into our lives to equip us for ministry and increase our ability to help others.

Blessed be the God and Father of our Lord Jesus Christ, the Father of mercies and God of all comfort, who comforts us in all our tribulation, that we may be able to comfort those who are in any trouble, with the comfort with which we ourselves are comforted by God. For as the sufferings of Christ abound in us, so our consolation also abounds through Christ. Now if we are afflicted, it is for your consolation and salvation, which is effective for enduring the same sufferings which we also suffer. Or if we are comforted, it is for your consolation and salvation. And our hope for you is steadfast, because we know that as you are partakers of the sufferings, so also you will partake of the consolation. (2 Corinthians 1:3-7)

God allows/brings storms into our lives to exhibit proof of our ministry.

But in all things we commend ourselves as ministers of God:

in much patience, in tribulations, in needs, in distresses. In stripes, in imprisonments, in tumults, in labors, in sleeplessness, in fastings; (2 Corinthians 6:4-5)

But you be watchful in all things, endure afflictions, do the work of an evangelist, fulfill your ministry. (2 Timothy 4:5)

God allows/brings storms into our lives to exhibit His love for us.

Who shall separate us from the love of Christ? Shall tribulation, or distress, or persecution, or famine, or nakedness, or peril, or sword? As it is written: "For Your sake we are killed all day long; We are accounted as sheep for the slaughter." Yet in all these things we are more than conquerors through Him who loved us. For I am persuaded that neither death nor life, nor angels nor principalities nor powers, nor things present nor things to come, nor height nor depth, nor any other created thing, shall be able to separate us from the love of God which is in Christ Jesus our Lord. (Romans 8:35-39)

God allows/brings storms into our lives to test our love for Him.

You shall not listen to the words of that prophet or that dreamer of dreams, for the LORD your God is testing you to know whether you love the LORD your God with all your heart and with all your soul. (Deuteronomy 13:3)

God allow/brings storms into our lives to perfect, establish, strengthen and settle us.

> But may the God of all grace, who called us to His eternal glory by Christ Jesus, after you have suffered a while, perfect, establish, strengthen, and settle you. (1 Peter 5:10)

God allows/brings storms into our lives so we learn from and cling to His Word.

> It is good for me that I have been afflicted, That I may learn Yourstatutes. Psalm (119:71)

God allows/brings storms into our lives to produce an irrefutable testimony.

> But before all these things, they will lay their hands on you and persecute you, delivering you up to the synagogues and prisons. You will be brought before kings and rulers for My name's sake. But it will turn out for you as an occasion for testimony. (Luke 21:12-13)

God allows/brings storms into our lives to give us the crown of life.

> Do not fear any of those things which you are about to suffer. Indeed, the devil is about to throw some of you into prison, that you may be tested, and you will have tribulation ten days. Be faithful until death, and I will give you the crown of life. (Revelation 2:10)

Ultimately, God allows/brings storms into our lives to prove that "all things work together for good".

> And we know that all things work together for good to those who love God, to those who are the called according to His purpose. (Romans 8:28)

If I have counted correctly, I have given you twenty-four reasons why God may unsettle your life even when it is not a result of your sins (except for chastisement). I am sure if you search the Scriptures you may come up with more. So, there is a lot of evidence as to why God operates in this fashion. But you may still be wondering WHY we need to endure these things anyhow. So, I close with two verses that hopefully will answer this question.

> For to this end we both labor and suffer reproach, **because we trust in the living God**, who is the Savior of all men, especially of those who believe. (1 Timothy 4:10, emphasis mine)

> Therefore let those who suffer **according to the will of God** commit their souls to Him in doing good, as to a faithful Creator. (1 Peter 4:19, emphasis mine)

CHAPTER 14

THE HYMNS OF PEACE

I chose to increase the impact of this book by just allowing you to bask in the peace found in many of our old hymns. This is a further effort to reinforce the ideas I have attempted to give you to bring peace into your life. Sing along, or at least hum the tunes if you know them, and let the truth of their messages flood your soul with peace.

IT IS WELL WITH MY SOUL
When peace like a river, attendeth my way, when sorrows like sea billows roll
Whatever my lot, Thou hast taught me to say, It is well, it is well with my soul.
It is well with my soul, it is well, it is well with my soul.

LIKE A RIVER GLORIOUS
Like a river glorious Is God's perfect peace, Over all victorious in its bright increase;
Perfect yet it floweth fuller every day, Perfect yet it groweth deeper all the way.
Trusting in Jehovah, hearts are fully blessed - Finding as He promised, Perfect peace and rest.

WONDERFUL PEACE
Far away in the depths of my spirit tonight, Rolls a melody sweeter than psalm.
In celestial-like strains it unceasingly falls O'er my soul like an infinite calm.
Peace, peace, wonderful peace, coming down from the Father above;
Sweep over my spirit forever I pray, in fathomless billows of love.

PEACE, PERFECT PEACE
Peace, perfect peace, in this dark world of sin?
The blood of Jesus whispers peace within
Peace, perfect peace, by thronging duties pressed:
To do the will of Jesus, this is rest.
Peace, perfect peace, with sorrows surging round?
On Jesus' bosom naught but calm is found.

THOU WILT KEEP HIM IN PERFECT PEACE
"Thou wilt keep him in perfect peace whose mind is stayed on Thee,"
When the shadows come and darkness falls, He giveth inward peace.
O He is the only perfect resting place, He giveth perfect peace!
"Thou wilt keep him in perfect peace whose mind is stayed on Thee."

ALL YOUR ANXIETY
Is there a heart o'er-bound by sorrow? Is there a life weighed down by care?
Come to the cross - each burden bearing, All your anxiety - leave it there.
All your anxiety all your care, Bring to the mercy seat - leave it there;
Never a burden He cannot bear, Never a friend like Jesus.

ALL THE WAY MY SAVIOR LEADS ME
All the way my Savior leads me - What have I to ask beside?
Can I doubt His tender mercy, Who through life has been my guide?
Heavenly peace, divinest comfort, Here by faith in Him to dwell!
For I know what-e'er befall me, Jesus doeth all things well;
For I know what-e'er befall me, Jesus doeth all things well.

HE HIDETH MY SOUL
A wonderful Savior is Jesus my Lord, A wonderful Savior to me;
He hideth my soul in the cleft of the rock, Where rivers of pleasure I see.
He hideth my soul in the cleft of the rock, That shadows a dry thirsty land,
He hideth my life in the depths of His love, And covers me there with His hand,
And covers me there with His hand.

THE HAVEN OF REST
My soul, in sad exile, was out on life's sea, So burdened with sin and distressed,
'Til I heard a sweet voice saying, "Make Me your choice,"
And I entered the haven of rest.
I've anchored my soul in the haven of rest, I'll sail the wide seas no more;
The tempest may rage o'er the wild stormy deep, In Jesus I'm safe evermore.

I KNOW WHO HOLDS TOMORROW
I don't know about tomorrow, I just live from day to day;
I don't borrow from its sunshine, For its skies may turn to gray.
I don't worry o'er the future, For I know what Jesus said;
And today I'll walk beside Him; For He knows what is ahead.
Many things about tomorrow I don't seem to understand;
But I know who holds tomorrow, And I know who holds my hand.

TRUSTING JESUS
Simply trusting everyday, Trusting through a stormy way;
Even when my faith is small, Trusting Jesus that is all.
Trusting as the moments fly, Trusting as the days go by;
Trusting Him what-e'er befall, Trusting Jesus, that is all.

'TIS SO SWEET TO TRUST IN JESUS
'Tis so sweet to trust in Jesus, Just to take Him at His word
Just to rest upon His promise, Just to know, "Thus saith the Lord."
Jesus, Jesus, how I trust Him! How I've proved Him o'er and o'er!
Jesus, Jesus, precious Jesus! O for grace to trust Him more!

ANYWHERE WITH JESUS
Anywhere with Jesus I can safely go.
Anywhere He leads me in this world below
Anywhere without Him dearest joys would fade,
Anywhere with Jesus I am not afraid.
Anywhere! Anywhere! Fear I cannot know;
Anywhere with Jesus I can safely go.

LEANING ON THE EVERLASTING ARMS
What a fellowship, what a joy divine, Leaning on the everlasting arms;
What a blessedness, what a peace is mine, Leaning on the everlasting arms.
Leaning, leaning, safe and secure from all alarms;
Leaning, leaning, Leaning on the everlasting arms.

JUST WHEN I NEED HIM MOST
Just when I need Him, Jesus is near, Just when I falter, just when I fear;
Ready to help me, ready to cheer, Just when I need Him most.
Just when I need Him most, Just when I need Him most;
Jesus is near to comfort and cheer, Just when I need Him most.

I MUST TELL JESUS
I must tell Jesus all of my trials, I cannot bear these burdens alone;
In my distress He kindly will help me, He always loves and cares
for His own.
I must tell Jesus! I must tell Jesus! I cannot bear these burdens alone;
I must tell Jesus! I must tell Jesus! Jesus can help me, Jesus alone.

HE GIVETH MORE GRACE

He giveth more grace when the burdens grow greater,
He sendeth more strength when the labors increase;
To added affliction He addeth more mercy,
To multiplied trials, His multiplied peace.
His love has no limit, His grace has no measure,
His power has no boundary known unto men;
For out of His infinite riches in Jesus,
He giveth, and giveth, and giveth again!

NO ONE UNDERSTANDS LIKE JESUS

No one understands like Jesus, He's a friend beyond compare;
Meet Him at the throne of mercy, He is waiting for you there.
No one understands like Jesus, When the days are dark and grim;
No one is so near, so dear as Jesus, Cast your every care on Him.

HE KEEPS ME SINGING

There's within my heart a melody - Jesus whispers sweet and low,
"Fear not, I am with thee - peace be still," In all of life's ebb and flow.
Jesus, Jesus, Jesus - sweetest name I know,
Fills my every longing, keeps me singing as I go.

WHAT A FRIEND WE HAVE IN JESUS

What a friend we have in Jesus, All our sins and griefs to bear.
What a privilege to carry, Everything to God in prayer.
Oh, what peace we often forfeit, Oh, what needless pain we bear.
All because we do not carry, everything to God in prayer.

GREAT IS THY FAITHFULNESS (Verse 3)

Pardon for sin and a peace that endureth,
Thine own dear presence to cheer and to guide,
Strength for today and bright hope for tomorrow,
Blessings all mine, with ten thousand beside.

Great is thy faithfulness, Great is thy faithfulness,
Morning by morning new mercies I see;
All I have needed Thy hand hath provided-
Great is Thy faithfulness, Lord, unto me.

If you have taken the time to read, and maybe sing along, then you can easily see these hymn writers of old knew how to find God's peace in any, and every situation life brought their way. They knew how to "stay their minds on Jehovah." The power music has should not come as a surprise since we saw how David playing his harp "refreshed the soul of Saul" (I Samuel 12:23). In fact, music can literally take you to a place where anger, guilt, anxiety, stress, etc. cannot live. But just in case you have not yet come to the place of peace in your life, the only advice that I can give you is to:

TURN YOUR EYES UPON JESUS
O soul, are you weary and troubled? No light in the darkness you see?
There's light for a look at the Savior, and life more abundant and free!
Turn your eyes upon Jesus, Look full in His wonderful face,
And the things of earth will grow strangely dim
in the light of His glory and grace.

CHAPTER 15

THE PEACE OF THE SHEPHERD

O nce again, I thought I had completed this book, but the Lord had other plans. My wife and I visited our granddaughter and her family in Goldsboro, NC and attended their church (The Bridge Church) on Sunday morning. Wouldn't you know it, the sermon stirred in me the need for at least one more chapter. I want to thank her pastors Jim Wall and Ryan Barbato for permission to use the sermon as the foundation for this addition to travel on "the path of peace". The sermon was about the Shepherd as found in Psalm 23:1 with references to the rest of the chapter which they will be preaching over the next few weeks.

Since we are on a path in the pursuit of peace, it is probably a good idea to find a Shepherd who can lead the way. So, let's take a look at this Shepherd, and how He can keep us on the path, keep us safe on the path, and keep us headed in the right direction. Remember who wrote this Psalm, that's right David, who was what before he became a king? That's right a shepherd, so he knew a lot about the shepherd and his relationship to his sheep.

This chapter regarding the Shepherd will focus on verse one and its implications for peace, but I believe it is essential that we keep the whole of Psalm 23 in mind as it relates to the aspects of who our Shepherd is, and what He can provide. So let us begin by simply reading the whole chapter as a starting point.

The LORD is my shepherd; I shall not want.
He makes me to lie down in green pastures; He leads me
beside the still waters.
He restores my soul; He leads me in the paths of righteousness
for His name's sake.
Yea, though I walk through the valley of the shadow of death,
I will fear no evil; For You are with me; Your rod and Your staff,
they comfort me.
You prepare a table before me in the presence of my enemies;
You anoint my head with oil; My cup runs over.
Surely goodness and mercy shall follow me All the days of my life;
And I will dwell in the house of the LORD Forever.

As we saw back in CHAPTER 2, the "person of peace" is none other than the Lord Jesus Christ, and as we see here in verse 1, He is our Shepherd as well. He is **"my"** Shepherd. In other words, He is Shepherd only to those who have accepted Him as their personal Savior. Therefore, we must belong to His flock, and then not only is He our Shepherd, but He is the **good Shepherd**.

"I am the good shepherd; and I know My sheep, and am known
by My own. As the Father knows Me, even so I know the Father;
and I lay down My life for the sheep." (John 10:14-15)

Next, we find in the first verse we **shall not want**, which is translated in some other versions of Scripture as **I have everything I need.** Mathew Henry puts it this way:

"From God's being his shepherd, he (David) infers that he shall not want anything that is good for him. See here the great care that God takes of believers…More is implied than is expressed, not only, *I shall not want*, but, I shall be supplied with whatever I need; and, if I have not everything I desire, I may conclude it is either not fit for me or not good for me, or I shall have it in due time" (pg. 257-8). So why do we worry and fret? Why do we sabotage our peace by not believing His Word and His promises to us?

This brings us to our first point. **The good Shepherd provides for His flock.** Even one of God's names (Jehovah-jireh) promises that "the Lord will provide". Has He not promised us:

And my God shall supply **all your need** according to His riches in glory by Christ Jesus. (Philippians 4:19, emphasis mine)

Those promises also include things like "grace and mercy to help in time of need" (Hebrews 4:16). Also, if you look at Matthew 6:25-32, we are told that since God cares for and provides for the birds, the lilies, even the grass, **how much more** does he care for you and me. In the context of this passage, we are then commanded to "not be anxious" for anything because our Shepherd "knows that we have need of all these things" we tend to worry about. Listen to Isaiah (40:29) as he speaks on this subject of God's provision:

He gives power to the weak, And to those who have no might He increases strength.

All of our needs, grace and mercy, necessities of life, power and strength, what more could be provided so we finally stop being anxious, quit worrying and stressing about life?

Charles H. Spurgeon comments thusly: "…the Lord is my Shepherd, he is able to supply my needs, and He is certainly willing to do so, for his heart is full of love, and therefore, "I shall not want". I shall not want for temporal things. I shall not want for spiritual things, I know that His grace will be sufficient for me" (pg 354).

The second thing we can note about the good Shepherd is that **He guides His sheep.** We see in Psalm 23:2-3 He leads us *beside still waters* and *in the paths of righteousness* which is one of the purposes of His rod and staff - to gently tap us and prod us in the right direction. Even when things are not going right in our eyes and afflictions come, *the Lord delivers the righteous out of them all* (Psalm 34:19). In fact, the promise is even more explicit:

> I will instruct you and teach you in the way you should go;
> I will guide you with My eye. (Psalm 32:8)

> When you pass through the waters, I will be with you; And through the rivers, they shall not overflow you. When you walk through the fire, you shall not be burned, Nor shall the flame scorch you. (Isaiah 43:2)

Not only guided, but instructed, and taught in the way we should go, guided by His own eye and His presence with us to protect us. How much safer can we be, and yet we worry!

In fact, not only does the Shepherd guide us, but He goes before us and even prepares the way.

> I will go before you and make the crooked places straight,
> I will break in pieces the gates of bronze and cut the bars
> of iron. (Isaiah 45:2)

However, there is a caveat to receiving the Shepherd's guidance.
> In all your ways **acknowledge him**, and he shall direct
> your paths. (Proverbs 3:6, emphasis mine)

I believe an old John W. Peterson song will emphasize the guidance of the Shepherd - *The Shepherd of Love*.

> Shepherd of love, you knew I had lost my way,
> Shepherd of love, you cared that I'd gone astray.
> You sought and found me, placed around me

Strong arms that carried me home;
No foe can harm me or alarm me-
Never again will I roam!
Shepherd of love, Savior and Lord and Guide,
Shepherd of love, forever I'll stay by your side.

The third thing to note about our good Shepherd is that **the Shepherd corrects His flock,** which is another purpose for his rod and staff. Is He a mean God? Why would he correct us? Quite the contrary, because He loves us He wants to not only guide us, but to keep us on the right path - the path that is for our good and His glory.

For whom the LORD loves He corrects, Just as a father the
son in whom he delights. (Proverbs 3:12)

For whom the LORD loves He chastens, And scourges
every son whom He receives, (Hebrews 12:6)

So, in love the shepherd corrects His flock for the following purpose:
For they indeed for a few days chastened us as seemed best
to them, but He **for our profit**, that we may be partakers of
His holiness. (Hebrews 12:10, emphasis mine)

Lastly, **the good Shepherd protects His flock**. This is a further purpose for His rod and staff. When I was younger, I remember hearing that in Biblical days a shepherd would sleep in the entrance to the fold. This served two protective purposes. One was to keep any sheep from wandering outside of the fold where it could get lost or be in harm's way from a wild animal. The second purpose was to keep a wild animal from entering the fold to harm any of the sheep.

Check out God's promise of protection and the reaction to it given by some of the prophets of the Old Testament.

No man shall be able to stand before you all the days
of your life; as I was with Moses, so I will be with you.
I will not leave you nor forsake you…the LORD your
God is with you wherever you go. (Joshua 1:5, 9)

Behold, God is my salvation, I will trust and not be
afraid; for Jehovah the LORD, is my strength and song;
He also has become my salvation. (Isaiah 12:2)

Fear not, for I am with you; be not dismayed, for I am
your God. I will strengthen you, yes I will help you,
I will uphold you with my righteous right hand.
(Isaiah 41:10)

Do not be afraid of their faces, for I am with you to
deliver you, (Jeremiah 1:8)

Then Isaiah combines the ideas of the Shepherd's provision and His
protection.

You have been a strength to the poor, A strength to
the needy in his distress, a refuge from the storm,
a shade from the heat… (Isaiah 25:4)

But I can hear some of you saying those guys were Israelites and
prophets called by God, so these promises don't apply to me. Are you
one of the flock? Have you accepted the Shepherd as Savior? Then you
too have been called by God, and as a member of His family fall under
the same protective hand.

Therefore remember that you, once Gentiles in the flesh–
who are called Uncircumcision by what is called the Circumcision
made in the flesh by hands– that at that time you were without

Christ, being aliens from the commonwealth of Israel and strangers from the covenants of promise, having no hope and without God in the world. **But now in Christ Jesus** you who once were far off have **been brought near** by the blood of Christ. For He Himself is our peace, who has made both one, and has broken down the middle wall of separation, having abolished in His flesh the enmity, that is, the law of commandments contained in ordinances, so as to create in Himself **one new man from the two**, thus making peace, and that He might **reconcile them both to God** in one body through the cross, thereby putting to death the enmity. And He came and preached peace to you who were afar off and to those who were near. **For through Him we both have access** by one Spirit to the Father.
(Ephesians 2:11-18, emphasis mine)

For in Christ Jesus neither circumcision nor uncircumcision avails anything, but **a new creation**. And as many as walk according to this rule, **peace and mercy be upon them**, and upon the Israel of God.
(Galatians 6:15-16, emphasis mine)

Do you remember I mentioned there was a caveat to receiving the guidance, provision, correction, and protection of the Shepherd? Just like the A, B, Cs of salvation (chapter 6), there are A, B, Cs for our relationship to the Shepherd as well.

A - accept Christ as Lord.

This is necessary to receive the benefits of having him as your Shepherd. Remember the verse which sparked the idea of a caveat?

In all your ways **acknowledge him**, and he shall direct your paths. (Proverbs 3:6, emphasis mine)

In the words of Matthew Henry: "We must not only in our judgment believe that there is an over-ruling hand of God ordering and disposing of us, and all our affairs, but we must solemnly own it…" (pg. 658). The Shepherd put it simply:

> If you love me, **keep my commandments**. He who has my commandments and **keeps them**, it is he who loves Me, and he who loves Me will be loved by my Father, and I will love him and **manifest myself to him**. (John 14:15, 21, emphasis mine)

> I am the good shepherd; and I know my sheep, and am known by my own…My sheep hear my voice, and I know them, and **they follow me**. (John 10:14, 27, emphasis mine)

So, the issue of lordship is not just a matter of salvation, but of obedience, and as an old saying goes: "obedience is the key to blessing".

> Oh, that you had **heeded My commandments! Then your peace** would have been like a river, And your righteousness like the waves of the sea. (Isaiah 48:18, emphasis mine)

B - be honest about your sin.

This means we not only confess our sin, but we reject it. We choose to believe and practice the truth of Romans 6 which tells us we are "free from sin". We also must believe there is no temptation above our ability to withstand it, and that God always makes a way to escape (I Corinthians 10:13). On this matter I recently heard a preacher on the radio put it this way: "Temptation is not a matter of what we do, but whom we love."

Most assuredly we are to confess our sins (I John 1:9), but even this is not mere verbal assent, but to truly agree with God about our sin, and God HATES sin. If we do not confess and reject our sin, then our relationship with the good Shepherd will suffer.

> He who covers his sins will not prosper, but whoever
> **confesses and forsakes** them will have mercy.
> (Proverbs 28:13, emphasis mine)

C - commit to community.

This means dedicating and using our gifts, talents, and abilities for the good of the body (the local flock) and for the furtherance of the Gospel to reach the unsaved. I believe I can best illustrate this point by quoting a couple of points from my local church's membership covenant.

> * To regularly participate in the life of Wellsboro Bible Church
> by attending weekly services, engaging in gospel-centered
> community, serving those within and outside this church,
> and evangelizing the lost (Acts 2:41-47, Hebrews 10:23-25,
> Titus 3:14)

> * To steward the resources God has given us, including time,
> talents, spiritual gifts, and finances. This includes regular
> financial giving, as well as service and participation in
> church that is sacrificial, cheerful, and voluntary
> (Matthew 25:14-30, Romans 12:1-2, 2 Corinthians 8-9,
> I Peter 4:10-11)

In those points, one Scripture reference seems to best summarize this commitment.

> And let us consider one another in order **to stir up love
> and good works.** Not forsaking the assembling of
> ourselves together, as is the manner of some, but
> **exhorting one another**, and so the much more as you
> see the day approaching. (Hebrews 10:24-25, emphasis mine)

So, to have the Shepherd as our shepherd, we must invite Him into our lives, claim Him as Lord, and serve the body. He is not only the good Shepherd, but also the *Gentle Shepherd,*

Gentle Shepherd, come and lead us, For we need You to help us find our way.
Gentle Shepherd, come and feed us, For we need Your strength from day to day.
There's no other we can turn to Who can help is face another day;
Gentle Shepherd, come and lead us, For we need You to help us find our way.

In summary, since the Lord is my Shepherd I do not have to worry, fret, or be anxious. I can be at peace because I can cast all my cares on the Shepherd, knowing that He cares for me (I Peter 5:7).

CHAPTER 16

THE PEACEFUL CONCLUSION

H aving read thus far, I trust you now agree with me that YOUR PEACE RESULTS MORE FROM YOUR ATTITUDE AND CONDUCT THAN FROM YOUR CIRCUMSTANCES. God's promises are true, He is faithful, and therefore, if peace is an elusive commodity in your life, you need to examine yourself as challenged by the Old Testament prophet Haggai.

> Now therefore, thus says the LORD of hosts: "Consider
> your ways! "You have sown much, and bring in little;
> You eat, but do not have enough; You drink, but you are
> not filled with drink; You clothe yourselves, but no one
> is warm; And he who earns wages, Earns wages to put
> into a bag with holes." (Haggai 1:5-6)

What a dismal picture of those who are seeking peace in material things, in their own manner, on their own terms. What a fruitless endeavor. Many even search for peace in "spiritual" things and decide as an act of their very own will to not do things God's way, much as did King David in a time of great emotional stress.

> In the day of my trouble I sought the Lord; My hand
> was stretched out in the night without ceasing;
> **MY SOUL REFUSED TO BE COMFORTED.**
> (Psalm 77:2, emphasis mine)

This verse highlights the fact that **our choice greatly affects our conduct and the outcome in our desperate search for peace.** This very same man of God had stated earlier:

> God is our refuge and strength, A very present help in
> trouble. (Psalm 46:1)

There you have it explained in the words of a "man after God's own heart" (I Samuel 13:14). Lack of peace is not God's fault but is the result of poor choices of will and action on our own behalf. We have met the greatest "enemy of peace", and **IT IS US**. Anytime we allow our minds to think about ourselves, our situations, our circumstances, figure out our own way, peace will disappear. How much rather we would:

> Be still, and know that I am God... (Psalm 46:10a)

Look at the apostle Paul's perspective about circumstances after he had "learned to be content" (Philippians 4:11), believed that "all things work together for good" (Romans 8:28), and decided "not to be anxious" (Philippians 4:6).

> We are hard-pressed on every side, yet **not crushed**;
> we are perplexed, but **not in despair**; persecuted,
> but **not forsaken**; struck down, but **not destroyed**.
> (II Corinthians 4:8-9, emphasis mine)

He did not have a "bed of roses" life after coming to know the Lord, and yet he had found God's grace was truly sufficient to meet any need of life. When writing this passage, he may have had in mind the following words of King David:

> Many are the afflictions of the righteous, But the
> LORD delivers him out of them all. (Psalm 34:19)

It is good for me that I have been afflicted, That I may
learn Your statutes. (Psalm 119:71)

His realization that God delivers from affliction, and that affliction
had a positive effect on him may have led David to pen one of the most
wonderful passages of scripture in all of God's Word. So peaceful is this
passage it needs to be repeated.

The LORD is my shepherd; I shall not
want. He makes me to lie down in green pastures;
He leads me beside the still waters. He restores my
soul; He leads me in the paths of righteousness For
His name's sake. Yea, though I walk through the
valley of the shadow of death, I will fear no evil;
For You are with me; Your rod and Your staff,
they comfort me. You prepare a table before me
in the presence of my enemies; You anoint my head
with oil; My cup runs over. Surely goodness and mercy
shall follow me All the days of my life; And I will dwell
in the house of the LORD Forever. (Psalm 23:1-6)

Peace like a river, green pastures beside still waters is what God
has in store for those who walk "the path of peace". Peace for any and
ALL of the storms of life is ours for the taking. Listen to a few words
from the chorus of the song "All Is Well" by Matt Huesmann and
Grant Cunningham.

"Peace is a place, a harbor safe
for riding out the storms…'

We can achieve this by simply "staying our minds" on the Lord and
by living in obedience to His Word. When our minds are stuck on the
negative focus (the black dot) you see neither God nor His gifts.

You will keep him in perfect peace, Whose mind is stayed
on You, Because he trusts in You. (Isaiah 26:3)

See how trust in God is the channel through which His peace flows.
Then thankfulness and right-thinking lift us up above our circumstances
to the place of peace which "surpasses all understanding" because
He is near.

Let your gentleness be known to all men. The Lord is at
hand. Be anxious for nothing, but in everything by prayer
and supplication, with thanksgiving, let your requests be
made known to God; and the peace of God, which surpasses
all understanding, will guard your hearts and minds through
Christ Jesus. Finally, brethren, whatever things are true,
whatever things are noble, whatever things are just, whatever
things are pure, whatever things are lovely, whatever things
are of good report, if there is any virtue and if there is anything
praiseworthy–meditate on these things. The things which you
learned and received and heard and saw in me, these do, and the
God of peace will be with you. (Philippians 4:5-9)

As we saw before, even a cursory reading of John chapter 14 presents
a very peaceful picture of how God relates to us and provides peace.
Think on these things:

Vss. 1-3 We have an eternal home.
Vs. 6 We have reconciliation through Christ.
Vss. 7-12 Christ is God, and all His promises are true and
available to us.
Vs. 13-14 We know our prayers will be answered in a way that
is best for us.
Vss. 15-26 We have His presence in our lives.
Vs. 27 We have the promise of HIS peace.

This is neatly and succinctly summed up by the Apostle Paul.
Now may the Lord of peace Himself give you peace
always in every way. The Lord be with you all.
(II Thessalonians 3:16)

Before I close, I would like to refer back to an old saying quoted in
chapter 8 and add to that an article which I just read online. The saying
was: "Sorrow looks back, worry looks around, but faith looks up." So,
check this out:

THE BUZZARD
If you put a buzzard in a pen that is 6 feet by 8 feet and is entirely open at
the top, the bird in spite of its ability to fly, will be an absolute prisoner.
The reason is that a buzzard always begins flight from the ground with
a run of 10 to 12 feet. Without space to run, as is its habit, it will not
even attempt to fly, but will remain a prisoner for life in a small jail
with no top.

THE BAT
The ordinary bat that flies around at night, a remarkable nimble creature
in the air, cannot take off from a level place. If it is placed on the floor or
ground, all it can do is shuffle about helplessly and, no doubt, pain- fully,
until it reaches some slight elevation from which it can throw itself into
the air. Then, at once, it takes off like a flash, but without that elevation,
it too would be a prisoner.

THE BUMBLEBEE
A bumblebee, if dropped into an open tumbler, will be there until it
dies, unless it is taken out. It never sees the means of escape at the
top, but persists in trying to find some way out through the sides near
the bottom. It will seek a way where none exists, until it completely
destroys itself.

PEOPLE

In many ways, we are like the buzzard, the bat, and the bumblebee. We struggle about with our problems and frustrations, never realizing that all we have to do is to look up! That's the answer, the escape route and the solution to any problem - just look up!

With this in mind: live simply, love generously, care deeply, speak kindly, and **trust in our God,** who loves us so deeply as to endue us with His peace.

An anonymous poem appeared in the *Church of England Magazine* on March 3, 1858. No one knows its author…It's a simple prayer, and perhaps its words will encourage you today…

> *Prince of Peace, control my will;*
> *Bid my struggling soul be still;*
> *Bid my fears and doubts to cease,*
> *Hush my spirit into peace.*
> *May Thy will, not mine be done;*
> *May Thy will and mine be one;*
> *Chase these doubtings from my heart,*
> *Now Thy perfect peace impart.*

"Peace is elusive in our world today, but we have the Prince of Peace with us, and He gives us His perfect peace. Let not your heart be troubled (John 14:1, 27). Ask Him today for His peace - and claim it" (Jeremiah, pg. 387).

In conclusion, see what is available: peace always, and peace in every way. No need for a single moment without peace; no situation in which peace cannot rule, for it is always there in every way. "Peace with God" and the "Peace of God" bringing peace into our hearts, minds, and consciences; peace in families, peace at work, peace in our churches, peace with all men, and peace in every situation. All this PEACE is available to you.

Finally, brethren, farewell. Become complete. Be of good comfort, be of one mind, live in peace; and the God of love and peace will be with you. (II Corinthians 13:11)

A peaceful prospect; a peaceful conclusion indeed! AMEN!!

ACKNOWLEDGEMENTS

First, I wish to thank my dear wife for the time writing this book has taken from our marriage. Her support of my ministries is a definite blessing from God. Next, I wish to thank my past Pastor, Rev. John Anderson (now deceased) and my friends Jan Johnston and Jill Tombs for the hours they have invested in proofing and critiquing the text. Lastly, thank you Rev. Charles Foster (now deceased) for the timely poem you shared with me and allowed me to include.

PEACE TO YOU ALL!

BIBLIOGRAPHY

Smith's Bible Dictionary (Uhrichville, OH: Barbour and Company, Inc,: 1987).

Merrill F. Unger, *Unger's Bible Dictionary* (Chicago, IL: Moody Press, 1980).

Reader's Digest, "Personal Glimpses", April, 1999, from Bill Bradley, *Values of the Game*, Artisan.

Victoria Neufeldt, Ed., *Webster's New World Dictionary* (New York, NY: Simon & Shuster, Inc., 1984).

W. E. Vine, *An Expository Dictionary of New Testament Words* (Nashville, TN: Royal Publishers, Inc.).

William Wilson, *Wilson's Old Testament Word Studies* (Peabody, MA: Hendrickson Publishers).

Joni Eareckson Tada, *Making Sense of Suffering*, Joni & Friends.

Joni Eareckson Tada, *Facing Trials With Joy*, Joni & Friends, 2007.

Matthew Henry, *Matthew Henry's Commentary*, Vol. 3 (Hendrickson Publishers, Inc., 1994)

C.H. Spurgeon, *The Treasury of David*, Vol. 1, (The Old Time Gospel Hour Edition,), (Thomas Nelson, Inc.)

Dr. David Jeremiah, *Strength For Today*, Turning Point, 2020

Dr. David Jeremiah, *The Book of Signs* (Nashville, TN: W Publishing, 2019) pg.87

Edward T Welsh, *Side By Side* (Wheaton, IL: Crossway, 2015)

All hymn words were taken from *Worship His Majesty*, (Alexandria, IN: Gaither Music Co., 1987)

ABOUT THE AUTHOR

D ennis Bliss grew up in a Christian home in a family that was dedicated to serving the Lord. He is married, a father, grandfather, and even a great-grandfather. After a couple of decades as a corporate accountant, God brought two life-changing trials into his life. Those trials did forever change the direction of his life, taking him from the field of accounting to marriage and family counseling. He got a Master's degree from Liberty University and opened Twin Tiers Christian Counseling Center in his hometown. He is an author, song writer, and recording artist who has traveled widely singing and speaking to the glory of God, and for the edifying of the men and women to whom he has ministered.

CPSIA information can be obtained
at www.ICGtesting.com
Printed in the USA
LVHW010045210922
728862LV00013B/461

9 781662 858246